A Guide College Survival

Revised Printing • 2014-2015

Jack Evans

Cover image © Shutterstock, Inc.

Kendall Hunt
publishing company

www.kendallhunt.com
Send all inquiries to:
4050 Westmark Drive
Dubuque, IA 52004-1840

Copyright © 2010 by Jack Evans

Revised Printing 2013.

ISBN 978-1-4652-5348-4

Kendall Hunt Publishing Company has the exclusive rights to reproduce this work,
to prepare derivative works from this work, to publicly distribute this work,
to publicly perform this work and to publicly display this work.

All rights reserved. No part of this publication may be reproduced,
stored in a retrieval system, or transmitted, in any form or by any means,
electronic, mechanical, photocopying, recording, or otherwise,
without the prior written permission of the copyright owner.

Printed in the United States of America
10 9 8 7 6

Disclaimer

Albeit the information contained within this book is current, accurate, and informative upon publication, the ultimate authority regarding academic policies, procedures, and graduation requirements is the current edition of your University Undergraduate Course Catalog and Academic Policies.

Contents

Beginning the Great Expedition—Your College Education 01
Welcome to the Biological Sciences 03
The Importance of Advising 05
The University and College of Science Curriculum and Liberal Education 09
Time Management, Study Skills, and Information-Processing Theory 13
Grades, Grades, Grades! 27
What do Former Undergraduates Have to Say about Their College Experience? 29
Which Way to Go? Pathways to Help Achieve Your Goals—Options 33
Honors Programs 43
Major Homework Assignments for College Survival and Life There After 45
Frequently asked Questions 71

BEGINNING THE GREAT EXPEDITION—YOUR COLLEGE EDUCATION

The purpose of *The Guide to College Survival* is to:

Provide a foundation through which students can achieve the goal of graduating from their chosen college or university, which will in turn lead to providing students with the tools necessary to be competitive applicants at the next level, such as graduate or professional school, and ultimately, the career of their choice.

At the end of this course, it will be expected that the students will:

1. Be able to navigate their way through the curriculum for the university, college, and department, and graduate on time with the courses and experiences that will make them competitive for their chosen career field.

2. Be able to change their academic direction without excessive course penalty.

3. Gain an awareness and appreciation for the resources, as well as academic and career advisors, available on this campus to aid in the academic and career decision-making process.

4. Have a greater awareness regarding the many opportunities available in the field of biology.

5. Have an increased appreciation and ability to present themselves as professional biologists. Freshman year is the right time to start a job search.

"Working It Out"
Camille Wright Miller
Reprinted with permission of *The Roanoke Times*

> **Q:** Our daughter looked for 10 months after college before finding her first job. That was too stressful; we'd like to spare our other children. Our son is a college junior. Other than declaring his major, he hasn't even started thinking about a job search. Can you provide guidelines so he (and we) can avoid a situation similar to his sister's?

A: Most successful students begin career efforts during their freshman year. Although he's behind, your son can make up for lost time.

First-semester freshman should make appointments with counselors in the college's career center. They should request an overview of services offered. A follow-up appointment should be made for assessment tests. These assessments will identify interests, preferences, possible majors, and possible careers.

During the second freshman semester, students should research summer internships. Every summer college students should be actively participating in internships within their chosen career. For those who need college funds, there are paid internships available. Internships provide an honest inside-the-career look, and are tremendous resume builders.

The junior year is the time to develop a resume, draft a cover letter, and continue researching careers. Juniors should talk with their advisor, their professors, and career counselors about possible opportunities. They should also attend college job fairs and continue with informational interviews.

First-semester seniors should be "on the market." They should be sending resumes to every possibility. They should be setting appointments with campus recruiters. Seniors should work to meet the goal of having desirable job offers by March.

Welcome to the Biological Sciences

Undergraduate biology curricula at the university level are designed to provide a broad education in the fundamentals of the discipline. These fundamentals provide the cornerstones necessary to allow students the opportunity to either continue their education in a graduate or professional school, or enter directly into the arena of being a professional biologist. In addition, it allows a selection of courses to prepare students for the health professions and for graduate training in ecology, genetics, microbiology, botany, zoology, molecular biology, and related fields. The Bachelor of Science degree in the biological sciences enables some students to initiate their careers immediately after graduation, while it gives others the opportunity to enter graduate or professional programs in various disciplines. The school's Department of Biological Sciences may also offer several unofficial tracks, which again will prepare a student for entry to graduate/professional schools or the biological career of their choosing.

Often times, a Bachelors of Science degree in the biological sciences can be awarded to students who satisfactorily complete their first three years of the curriculum in biology and the first year of work in an accredited school of medicine, dentistry, veterinary medicine, or pharmacy school. Students may wish to seek out an academic advisor to see if such possibilities exist at their institution and if they are suitable.

What Is a Biologist?

Typically, when I ask people this question, I get a variety of answers. The lay public often has a skewed view of the multitude of components responsible for making a biologist. Therefore, I often receive answers describing what a biologist is that conform to how social media portray a biologist. Typically, the first thing that comes to mind is *Animal Planet.* One could argue that it is true—many of the people on *Animal Planet* are trained as biologists. But, one must ask what are the parts that create the whole?

Biologists need to be well versed in a whole host of disciplines. For much of my biological career, I was involved in aquatic biological systems. The disciplines I needed to be successful at what I did were many. Biology, both organic and inorganic chemistry, physics, as well as statistics were all very important tools I needed to have in my toolbox so-to-speak relevant to my research.

I mention this because this is precisely the curriculum that you are about to enter, whether to do aquatic research or not. All biologists need to be well versed in the aforementioned disciplines. Therefore, the curriculum will in part reflect many of these associated disciplines. Prior to signing on the dotted line saying they are going to major in biology, it is imperative that students first check out the curriculum required for a bachelor's degree in the biological sciences.

Academic Planning

Students have considerable flexibility in the choice of biology and free electives when designing their individual programs of course work because most universities have numerous biology electives. This flexibility often times allows a student to take courses tailor-made for them and their career aspirations. Freshmen and transfer students often are required to enroll in a college success–type course designed to help them begin their academic and career planning. Also, students are assigned an academic advisor to help them design a program of study that will meet their academic and career goals.

All science departments, regardless of the institution, will have a departmental website that is continuously updated. These websites are rich sources of information related, in part, to the topics listed below.

- **Departmental Academic Information**
  - Departmental Requirements
  - Biology Curriculum Check Sheets
  - Advising Information
- **Calendars**
  - Upcoming Seminars, Workshops
  - Job Opportunities and Summer Internships
  - Study Abroad Opportunities
  - Scholarship Opportunities
  - Upcoming Events and Deadlines
- **Biology Advisors and Faculty Information**
  - Faculty Research Interests
  - Links to Faculty Web Pages and Their Areas of Research Interest

The department offers many opportunities, but successful completion of an undergraduate program requires the student to take a proactive initiative to develop and maintain an academic program, and to seek out the help of appropriate advisors and resources within and outside the department.

Students are accountable for their individual progress and success. This is *your* education.

The Importance of Advising

The cover of this book was purposely chosen. The diagram represents a compass. You need a "compass" to help navigate your way through the many decisions you will have to make while a biology student at your chosen institution, in order to graduate on time with the courses and experiences you will need to be a successful candidate to enter whatever field you choose.

As such, your compass should be pointed toward valuable assets such as good academic and career advisors. This person or persons may or may not be one of your professors. Some students frequently see more than one advisor. Regardless of whether you have only one advisor or more than one, seeking guidance from professional people on campus is an important way to ensure your academic success.

There exist many definitions of advising: with that said, advising, if done properly, is a ***collaborative process*** between the student and his or her advisor. This collaborative process will lead to the exchange of information that encourages the individual student to make responsible academic and career decisions. Note the emphasis on "collaborative process." This process requires that you, the student, take the initiative to cultivate a working relationship with your advisor. This relationship will in turn help you make wise and timely decisions regarding your academic and career plans. With that said, students should make a concerted effort each semester, prior to course request, to visit with their academic advisor to help ensure that they are enrolling in the appropriate courses for the upcoming semester for their chosen career path.

When Is the Right Time to See My Advisor?

Since your advisors, both academic and career, are some of your greatest assets here on campus, the right time to see them is anytime that you have questions or concerns. More pointedly, you should meet with your advisor(s) at least one time every semester. That is just prior to course request, as it is of utmost importance that you are fulfilling all of your requirements for a BS degree in the Biological Sciences, and that you are taking courses that are important for your success later in life. These meeting times can and should be used to:

➤ *Understand* fully the course requirements needed to fulfill a BS in the Biological Sciences;

➤ *Evaluate* the scope of biological science courses possible for you to take, and plan accordingly.

Advisors are skilled professionals who are aware of all academic policies and procedures, as well as graduation requirements necessary for student success. To that end, you and your advisor(s) hold the key to success. Therefore, you should seek his or her advice whenever needed.

It may be that, for whatever reason, you are not able to meet with your advisor in a face-to-face meeting. If this is the case, an email is often an acceptable way to voice your concerns and ask your questions. With that said, it must be done in a professional manner. Therefore, your email must be professionally formatted because you are now in an environment that dictates that you express your thoughts in a professional voice.

When Is the Right Time to Meet My Professors?

I always tell my students to meet their professors after class on the first day. It is critically important that students take the time to meet their professors. By doing so, you will make a lasting impression on your professor because you are exhibiting your professionalism, maturity, and civility, and that you are interested in the course in question. Also of great importance is to take advantage of your professor's office hours throughout the semester. Again, going to see a professor during office hours shows your interest in the course at hand.

While meeting and getting to know your professors may seem insignificant, it is of vital importance for at least two reasons. First, if you are having issues with the course in question, for whatever reason, your professor will be able to address said issues. Teaching is part of our jobs, and most of us love what we do and are passionate about the material in the courses we teach. We share that passion with our students, both in the classroom and during one-on-one visits when students come to see us during our office hours. If you are unable to attend your professors' office hours, all you will need to do is to contact them via email and set up an alternative meeting time.

As professors, we find it very frustrating at the end of the semester when a student has earned an unflattering grade (D's and F's). If only these students would have come to see us during our office hours to get the help they needed, perhaps instead of D's and F's, the students in question would be receiving A's and B's. It is all up to the student. Remember, this is *your* education.

There is another very important reason to get to know your professors. While you are an undergraduate, many of you will be applying for scholarships. Also, once you come to the end of your journey as an undergraduate, you will be applying to graduate school, professional schools such as medical school, or entering the work force. All of these ventures will require that you have letters of recommendation. Often, at least three letters of recommendation are needed, and one or two of them will necessarily need to come from your college professors. Therefore, it is imperative that you get to know at least one or two of your professors! Letters of recommendation carry a significant amount of weight in the application process, regardless of whether it is for scholarships, graduate school, medical school, or the work force.

Below are two emails that I received literally days apart from each other; they illustrate the importance of getting to know your professors. The emails were not edited, other than to add bold font to emphasize some very important points.

Hey Dr. Evans,

*I had two quick questions for you and I need some advice, if you wouldn't mind. I am a Biological Sciences major and I am in the process of applying for the College of Science scholarship. As I began filling out the College of Science scholarship (I am out of state, so my parents are really pushing me to get scholarships, as you can understand!) I saw that I had to put **a professor or advisor's email address down for a letter of reference**. This left me stumped because I didn't know who to put. **I know that from the first day of school we are told to get to know our professors and I admit that I could have done a better job at that**. However, **I didn't really need to attend professor's office hours** for help last semester because I understood the material (I got a 4.0 GPA last semester). **I sometimes went to my professor's office hours to get questions answered but I didn't form relationships with the professors**. In conclusion, I have not been able to form relationships with my advisors either, because I haven't consistently met with the same person. Therefore, I was just wondering if you could give me advice on how I should have been forming relationships with professors and advisors, and how I should for the future so that I will be able to get to know my professors and advisors better and have the opportunity to get reference letters.*

Thank you so much for your time.

Dear Dr. Evans,

My name is XXXX. You may remember me from your biology seminar during fall semester.

*I wanted to ask you a question about the College of Science Scholarship Application. The due date for the application is March 1st, as you probably know. However, I have been delaying my application due to the need of a completed FAFSA form, which caused more trouble than anticipated. As the deadline has approached, **I noticed the need for a reference to a professor or advisor who will be willing to supply a Letter of Support**. You are more than likely familiar with the process, but I would like to ask you if you would be interested in being my reference. I am currently enrolled at Virginia Tech as a Biology and Chemistry Major. As a freshman student in many large, general classes, **it has been very difficult to get to know many professors very well on a personal level**. I can understand if you would prefer not to, but I hope you will consider reading a little bit of personal information about me to give you a better idea of who I am.*

As is evident, from the above emails, getting to know your professors is of critical importance. Both of the above students missed potential scholarship opportunities because they did not take the initiative to form a relationship with any of their professors. Hopefully, they now have both learned the importance of becoming acquainted with their professors.

Again, this is your education. You will get from it exactly what you put into it. If you know your faculty well, they in turn can and will construct a strong letter of recommendation for you. Conversely, if your professors do not know you, as the above examples show, they cannot write you a strong letter of recommendation. Without strong letters of recommendation from faculty that know you well, it will be difficult to be competitive at the next level, whether that is a seat in graduate/professional programs and/or the scientific workforce, or, as represented by the above examples, receiving a scholarship to help pay for your college education. As such, it is up to you, the student, to forge these positive relationships with your faculty.

A Philosophy for Learning

Faculty and students have a *joint* responsibility for the learning process.

Faculty members are responsible for guiding inquiry to help develop in students the ability to think critically, communicate effectively, and become contributing citizens to a democratic society. It is also our jobs as faculty to challenge students. This in turn creates a well-educated member of society.

That said, students are responsible for making themselves available to, and to embrace, the learning process, for actively engaging in the learning dialogue, and for taking advantage of the many opportunities in an institution where ideas, exploration, and free expression are so highly valued.

In summary, students are responsible for developing a positive attitude about self-education and self-worth; in other words, you must take ownership of your education. Learning goes beyond simply taking tests and receiving a grade. Learning is a participatory, active process of inquiry, questioning, and intellectual exploration. For the university-educated student, the love of learning should be a lifelong activity. Your educational experience (kindergarten through high school) prior to coming to college was mandated. Higher education, on the other hand, is a privilege. This is *your* education, and that means *you* should take ownership of it.

The University and College of Science Curriculum and Liberal Education

Students graduating with a university degree must have breadth and depth in their education. Therefore, they must have a connection to the past and present in the form of cultural heritage, an opportunity to develop crucial intellectual skills, and an introduction to the issues that our society will face in the twenty-first century. All of these potential connections are at your disposal upon entering a university.

These issues include, but are not limited to, morals and ethics, and cultural, racial, political and gender-based diversity issues; the effects of technology, specifically biotechnology, in society; as well as environmental crises and issues that relate to our sustainability on Planet Earth. Therefore, while you are completing your science requirements, you will also need to be well versed in topics outside your chosen discipline, such as many of those listed above. Worldly issues rarely, if ever, encompass only a single discipline. So, a well-rounded education is imperative. Since you will be wearing the tunic of an educated person, society will turn to you for creative solutions to its problems. That said, you must be prepared because the world will be looking to *you* for solutions to life's most pressing issues.

University and College Requirements at the Undergraduate Level, Regardless of the College or University, Have Been Designed to Ensure That Each Student Will:

1. Receive a broadly based foundation of knowledge outside his or her area of specialization.
2. Gain knowledge of, and competence in, using analytic and creative problem-solving processes.
3. Develop a global perspective about the diversity of human experience and knowledge.
4. Understand how diverse intellectual skills and knowledge can be used to solve complex problems.

5. Acquire valuable skills in communicating ideas using numbers, words, and speech.
6. Develop skills of critical thinking as it relates to culture, values, information, and ideas.
7. Develop the habit and love for lifelong learning and the ability to respond to new ideas.

In charting your course, remember to include both University Core Requirements and College Core Requirements. At times, the two are one and the same. In other cases, an individual college may have a slight modification of university requirements. Because you are in the College of Science, it is important that you know the specific requirements as they apply to your college.

One of My Former Students Says ... "Success"
Goal Setting

This step takes a good bit of introspection. Students must be absolutely certain that the academic path they plan to undertake is one of their own making and not dictated from outside sources. This statement may seem straightforward enough, but it is of great importance. I say this because I have heard too many times students say, "I am planning on going to medical school after I graduate." When I probe a little further, I find out the student doesn't wish to go to medical school, but rather his or her parents wish it. *Do not* fall into this trap! Remember, this is *your* education and *your* life, and no one else's. If your desire is there and is genuine, then the foundations have been laid for success.

The next step is to define (on paper) your long-term goals and short-term objectives; get used to recording everything. At the end of the day, you should ask yourself what you have accomplished. Make sure the answer is a positive one.

Success Gravitates toward Success

The people with whom you associate are a reflection of you. Additionally, these people act as a strong influence on you; therefore, make certain that your peers have ambitious goals that coincide with yours. Again, your goal is to be a scientist; otherwise, you would not have chosen the major that you did. That said, it is most advantageous to establish a rapport with a faculty member who can be a source of guidance, especially during difficult periods.

Turn Failures into Victories

A poor performance on one test should be used to improve rather than hinder performance on following tests. Understand why you did not do as well as you wanted to do, and then act accordingly; fix whatever needs to be fixed prior to the next exam. To find out how to do this, take advantage of your professors' office hours. Professors are here for you, so take advantage of what they have to offer. Preparation is the key to tackling any difficult exam; if you find that your preparation scheme is not working in a particular circumstance, then modify it, again, with the consultation/aid of the professor or teaching assistant for the course in question.

These general guidelines have served me well over the last few years. I do not believe in getting too detailed in methodology because that is best suited for the individual to construct based on his or her personal preferences. Each student must find what works best, academically speaking, and then act accordingly.

Another Former Student Says …
"Fraternity"

I was in the Biology Orientation Seminar for biology majors last semester and just wanted to give next year's freshmen some advice. Here goes.

I came from high school with a 3.7 GPA and did not have to work a second to even get it. I arrived at college and still had that attitude a little. I got wrapped up with pledging a fraternity and thought I could pull myself up again after slipping far below my usual standards. Little did I know, it was too late. Now I am paying the price this summer. Being on academic probation, I have to work double the amount I would have had to if I had put forth even a little effort last semester, and I have no room for screw-up's. I cannot overemphasize the importance of not getting behind. Do not find out the hard way as I did.

On a side note, I did find the class very helpful. I just wish that I would have had the common sense at the time to use some of the help and resources that were spoken about during the class.

Time Management, Study Skills, and Information-Processing Theory

Being accepted to college, as you know, is not an easy task. It requires, among other things, a stellar high school GPA, which, for incoming biology students at the university in which I teach, averages approximately 3.9 on a 4.0 scale from year to year. You have been accepted to college and, therefore, should be proud of your accomplishments thus far, because, academically speaking, you are one of the best of the best, as reflected in part by your high school achievements. Therefore, you were invited here because we think that you have what it takes academically speaking to be successful at the college level. Prior to entering college, my guess is that your high school experience was much like mine. Most incoming students (freshman as well as transfer students) have never seen a C on either their exams or report cards during their previous 12 to 16 years of education.

My experience over the years has been that many students entering college have found that high school and/or community college came relatively easy to them, and therefore, they may not have been overly challenged regarding their academics. Also, prior to coming to a four-year institution of higher education, many students have had the luxury of living at home. My guess is that there were many benefits to this plan, such as help from family with cooking meals, doing laundry, getting out of bed in a timely fashion to make it to school, and so forth. As a rule, students prior to entering a four-year institution had a very balanced life including, but not limited to, personal, social, family, work, and lastly academics. Consequently, students entering a four-year institution have a very high level of confidence. It is imperative that this confidence level remain high.

Upon entering the arena of a four-year institution, many students will experience some culture shock. College life is often times very different from what the typical student has experienced to this point. Many comforts of home are gone, and the academic bar often times will be significantly higher than it was set at the high school or community college level, which may lead to a serious issue I call the "first semester blues." This issue of the first semester blues often times results from the absence of two vital ingredients that promote college success—time management and study skills. Without these very important tools, students may find it difficult to get to the end of the journey—a Bachelor of Science degree from the Department of Biological Sciences of their chosen four-year institution. Therefore, this section is designed in hopes of providing some valuable examples and ideas to help navigate around the "first semester blues."

Make a Schedule

It is generally accepted that most college students at a four-year institution should plan to spend approximately two to three hours outside of the classroom studying, writing papers, and doing projects and the like for every hour spent inside the classroom. To that end, a student who takes 15 hours of course work and puts in at least 30 hours of related work per week is looking at a 45-hour workweek as it relates to the demands of college. That being the case, students may need a schedule to help balance their academic life while in college. Examinations, presentations, research papers, homework, not to mention all of the other things that will be part of everyday existence at school, require that students organize their lives. To this end, if you choose to create a schedule, you may want to address several issues when making said schedule, such as the following.

Identify Those Things That Waste Your Time

This is something of which we are all guilty! These time-wasters as they relate to academics come in all shapes and sizes; maybe you are sleeping 12 hours a day, or are playing video games daily for hours at a time. Perhaps you have outside employment. A schedule that will help you manage your time can be a very valuable tool. In order to make the best use of your time, noting that you have at least a 45-hour academic workweek, you need to identify and eradicate those things that are not doing anything positive for you; eliminating them will allow you the opportunity to become more productive. This does not mean, by any stretch of the imagination, that you want to completely do away with your fun activities; these are vitally important as well. It is very important to have an outlet for the stresses that can accompany attending a four-year institution. This outlet comes in the way of making sure you are taking time for yourself, which in turn will relate to your physiological well being. This in turn will allow you to perform, academically speaking, at your best.

What Is Your Most Productive Time of the Day?

It is important to know when you are at your best, and plan accordingly. Plenty of research studies suggest that some, though not all, people are much more efficient during certain hours of the day than others. Therefore, if you find that your most productive time to do out-of-class schoolwork is at five in the morning, then so be it! Plan your day accordingly. While in college, we all have, to a degree, the opportunity to choose the time of day in which we take our courses in any given semester. This is where being aware of your biological clock, also known as your circadian rhythms, becomes important relevant to student success in the classroom. In short, all organisms—whether we are talking about broccoli or human beings—all organisms have circadian rhythms. Circadian rhythms are based roughly on a 24-hour cycle in biochemical, physiological, or behavioral processes.

As mentioned earlier, much research has been done on circadian rhythms, learning styles, and the existing relationship between time of day and student learning. Further, much of this research suggests that when students find their most productive time of day and schedule their classes and studying accordingly, there is a strong correlation with increases in overall GPAs.

That said, the "best" time to learn may be different for everyone. Some students may be most productive with early morning courses, while others may prosper with afternoon or evening courses. Therefore, it is of critical importance for students to know when they are most productive and create a semester course schedule that is most conducive to success, in and out of the classroom.

The Order of Your Schedule

Once you have identified what wastes your time and when you are most productive, you then need to think about the order of your schedule. The sequence in which you accomplish things is important to consider when creating a schedule. What I am about to tell you may seem counterintuitive: You will want to schedule your most difficult subjects or the ones you enjoy the least first, during your most productive time of the day. The rationale here is simple. Whether you like it or not, you must complete the work. Therefore, complete your most unsavory task first, and save the work you are most excited about to do last. It is much more likely that you will be motivated to work on a subject that you really enjoy. Conversely, it is less likely that you will be motivated to work on something you are not that crazy about. Therefore, get the one that you are not crazy about doing out of the way first, as the motivation will still be there later for the subject that you like.

Make Use of "Downtime"

Remember that the name of the game is to maximize the use of your time. You may have an hour or two between classes, or no classes at all on a particular day. If you use these times to sleep, play video games, watch TV, update your FaceBook account, and download music from the internet, you may not be using your time productively, especially if these are cognitively your most productive hours of the day.

In the stressful world of being a college student, the appropriate use of "downtime," or time out of the classroom, is very important. Doing some of the things you enjoy helps control the stresses of a demanding college curriculum, such as what we typically find in the biological sciences. The take-home message here is that a little downtime is a good thing, but a lot of downtime can be a sure-fire way to find yourself experiencing the "first semester blues," which is not where you want to be!

Your Schedule Only Works If You Use It!

Remember that if you create a schedule for yourself, it is just that—a schedule. What I mean by this is that schedules are only effective if you use them. So, if you create a schedule, make sure that you give it a chance to work. Once you have given it a test drive, so to speak, you may find that it is perfect the way it is, it may need some minor adjustments, or it plain and simply does not work. What I do know is that you will never know whether it works or not unless you give it a try.

Sleep, Nutrition, and Hygiene

When planning your schedule, you cannot forget some of the basics of life—sleep, food, and cleanliness. My experience, both as an undergraduate student and as a college faculty member, is that, as a rule, students do not get enough sleep and or lack proper nutrition. Sleep and food for students are akin to gas and oil for automobiles. If cars do not have the proper gas and oil, they will not work properly. They will break down and then must be taken to the mechanic. Our bodies work the same way, but instead of gas and oil, they need sleep and food. Without the proper amount of sleep and food, a student cannot work at his or her best, and may get sick and have to go to the doctor.

Your parents have more than likely been telling you for years that you need to get a good night's rest and that you need to eat right—whatever that means. Truth be told, your parents have been giving you very sound advice! Turns out that there is a large quantity of scientific research and literature that validates what your parents have been telling you all these years. Research has shown that sleep is a vital function in regard to recuperation and regeneration throughout the body, and particularly, the brain.

This recuperative sleep, or lack thereof, plays an important role in learning and memory. Research has shown that learning may actually take place during recuperative sleep, as the brain consolidates and practices what we have learned during the day. Further research has documented that subjects deprived of sleep lack the abilities to make quick and/or logical decisions. Also, studies have shown that those deprived of sleep do not perform as well on tests, when compared to subjects who have received an adequate amount of sleep.

I often hear from students that they stayed up all night long studying for an exam. As a rule, they also have a tendency to say that they were not pleased with the results of said exam. While pulling an "all-nighter" studying for an exam may seem like a rite of passage, it fails in comparison with someone who has been studying a little each day and then gets a quality night's sleep prior to the exam. With that said, when it comes to pulling an all-nighter, *just say no*! Research shows that there is a much better way to do things if your goal is to learn the material.

Proper nutrition is a must for a whole host of reasons concerning the proper functioning of the body, but relevant to this discussion is the relationship of glucose and the brain as it relates to learning. Glucose is the major fuel used by the body and brain. When we ingest carbohydrates, they are broken down by a variety of processes and eventually make their way, as glucose, to the bloodstream, and thus, become available for the body and brain to use as fuel. Of critical importance here is that glucose is not stored. As such, the brain is dependent for its energy on the available glucose in the blood stream. With that said, it is critically important that we maintain our glucose level needs throughout the day in order to supply the appropriate energy to the body and brain. At this point, it should go without saying that if our glucose levels drop, our brains cannot function at an optimal level.

There is a large amount of evidence in the available research that suggests that low glucose levels have a negative effect on cognitive processes, such as memory and comprehension. As a result, appropriate glucose levels are not only important for helping create memories but also for storing memories. Several studies, using undergraduates as research subjects, show that students with adequate blood glucose levels significantly outperformed students with lower blood glucose levels in multiple-choice exams.

While this is only one example, a significant amount of research in the scientific world demonstrates modest increases in blood glucose concentration levels enhance learning and memory. The moral of the story here is one that your parents have been telling you for years. And that is to make sure you eat breakfast, lunch, and dinner, as well as have a snack or two throughout the day. If you do this, your chances of performing at a high academic level will increase when compared to not having an appropriate dietary intake of glucose. As we shall see, glucose is not the only nutrient that the body and brain need to function at their optimum level.

Glucose Is Important, but We Need More...

As noted earlier, glucose plays a very important role in relation to optimal brain performance. Research also shows that more than just adequate levels of glucose are important in order for our cognitive processes to function at their best. Research indicates that diets rich in protein also have a positive effect on memory performance. Many studies have tested two research groups, one with a protein-rich diet and one with a protein-deficient diet. These studies have clearly shown that those with a protein rich-diet perform much better on memory tests than those with a diet deficient in protein.

Glucose and Protein Are Important, but We Need More

Yes, glucose and protein are important, but it turns out there is more to it than that. Again, research has shown that diets high in vitamins C, E, A, and the B complex, just to name a few, are responsible for increased mental cognition. Many studies have concluded that deficiencies of essential nutrients, such as the vitamins just mentioned, result in failing memory and poor concentration. So, the moral of the story here is to make sure that you have a balanced diet. A balanced diet in turn will allow our brains to function at their best. College life demands that our brains are working optimally all the time. For this to happen, a balanced diet is a necessity.

Staying Clean

Another thing that we all must keep in mind, as silly as it may sound, is something that our parents have said to us over and over again as we were growing up. I can still hear my mother saying, "Make sure you wash your hands." As simple as it sounds, this statement is incredibly important here at Virginia Tech. Since we are all biologists, this statement should make perfect sense. Think about it. You are in a new place, as are the other 25,000 students here on campus. Each of us brings with us a variety of viruses, bacteria, and the like. Some of these things, your body has previously encountered. If so, your immune system "remembers" these pathogens and will more than likely wipe them out before they have a chance to propagate and make you sick. Since you are surrounded by 25,000 or so new people, you can guarantee that other students have brought with them a whole host of pathogens that you and your immune system have never met before. This is where there is potential for trouble, unless of course we heed the well-thought-out advice of our parents and make sure we wash our hands.

Just think about a typical large lecture a room which seats as many as 550 students during any given class. Everyone has to open the door to enter class. Sooner or later, after you have entered the classroom, you will eat some food or touch your face, and many of the pathogens that were on the door handle have the potential of entering your body. If you wash your hands on a regular basis, most of these nasty pathogens will be killed and/or removed. If you do not wash them, the pathogens have an open invitation to enter your body and potentially wreak havoc. What you must be aware of is: the university and your workload will not stop or decrease because you are sick or not functioning at your best. Therefore, the moral of this story is to get an adequate amount of sleep, eat a healthy diet, and wash your hands often. Again, this is *your* education, and if you are stuck in your dorm room sick, it will pass you by.

Summing It All Up

As you can see, there are many variables that must be used in regard to becoming the best learner that you can be. Further, these variables of success are not just hearsay, but are backed by sound research in biology, psychology, and education. By incorporating time-management strategies, the use of schedules, revamping your study skills if need be, as well as employing proper sleep, nutrition, and hygiene, you will become a better student and you will receive higher grades. This in turn will allow you a greater opportunity to secure a seat in graduate or medical school or get that job you have always dreamed of having. If you choose to follow this advice, you will be amply rewarded. Conversely, if you choose not to, then you may not achieve, academically speaking, what you feel you should. The moral of the story is that *it is up to you!*

What Do I Do to Prepare Myself for Class?

This is fairly intuitive, but with that said, I am surprised how many students do not adequately prepare themselves for class. The first answer to this all-important question is very easy: attend class—not just some, but all of your classes. This idea may seem very obvious and should go without saying. The reason I mention it is because you will not receive all the information you need to do well just by reading and obtaining notes from a class that you have missed. Remember that your professors are experts in their chosen field. Therefore, they are on the cutting edge of the current research in said field, some of which will not be printed in textbooks for years to come. So, by attending all classes, you will ensure that you will not miss any pertinent information related to the subject at hand.

The second answer to this question is to read the assigned chapters in your book prior to coming to class. All professors hand out a syllabus and, more or less, will follow it. Deep learning, as you will find out from the information-processing passage, comes from practice. Your first opportunity to practice and make yourself familiar with the subject matter is to read before attending class.

At least two important ideas need to be considered when reading. One is that text books are packed with terminology that may be somewhat foreign to the student. As such, it is important to develop your vocabulary for the course in question. I teach biology, and most all of the terms we, as biologists, use are Greek or Latin. Therefore, most students are truly learning a new language when they enter one of my courses. Ergo, it is a good idea to make flash cards to learn these new words and definitions. Science textbooks almost always have a glossary in the back with definitions. Also, the student has many other tools at his or her disposal, such as the internet, the library, other students, and, most importantly, their professors.

Second, students may want to get in the habit of highlighting important concepts in their books. At first glance, it may seem that *everything* in the book is "important," and to a degree, that is true, otherwise the author would not have included it in the book. I would like to suggest that you do not highlight anything until you have read the whole passage. Once you have read the passage and found what you think is of importance, you may want to then highlight key words or phrases in said passage. Reading prior to class, highlighting important material, and making flash cards of important terms will provide you the practice necessary to 1) be familiar with the material during lecture, and 2) start to prepare you for the impending exam which you will be confronted with in the near future. Education equals practice, and practice equals education.

What Do I Do While in Class—Listening and Taking Notes!

Listening and taking notes. Wow, that seems like a no-brainer. There is at least one thing that can interfere with this otherwise apparently easy task. This one thing is your computer. Only bring your computer if you are going to use it constructively, in other words, *only* if you are going to take notes with it, thus using it as a tool for learning. I have seen many times that students bring their computers to class with good intentions only to become distracted by checking their emails or Facebook. Before they know it, class is over and they have very little to show for it. Sure, their emails have been answered and their Facebook page has been updated, but they have taken very few notes pertaining to the subject at hand.

At the end of the semester, it is inevitable that I have students come to see me and say that they did not receive the grade in my course(s) that they could have otherwise achieved. The primary culprit typically is bringing their computer to class. Therefore, if you are going to bring your computer to class, use it as a tool that that will allow you to take great notes and thereby help you in learning the material at hand. In turn, you will be better prepared to take exams and get the final grade in the course that you deserve.

Should I Try to Write Down Everything the Professor Says?

The easy answer here is no. There is no need to attempt to write down everything the professor says. It can be counterproductive for a couple of reasons.

1. Not everything we say as professors is worthy of writing down.
2. It is physically impossible to write down everything we say. So, if you try to write it all down, it is inevitable that you will miss some truly important information that you should capture.
3. By trying to write everything down you will not be an active listener and again you will probably be missing some important information that the professor is trying to impart unto the class.

Reading the book, as noted prior, is essential. That said, it should be known that the material in your book is important, but your professors are often on the cutting edge of the research pertaining too many of the topics in your book. Therefore, it is not out of the ordinary for your professors to introduce new cutting-edge research in science that your book does not cover. That said, active listening is important.

There are many different strategies when it comes to taking notes, such as the *Cornell note-taking method, Two-column method, REAP strategy, and the Form strategy*, just to name a few. It will be important for your success in college to review the many different methods available and find the one that works best for you.

Again, we learn through practice, and that practice comes in many forms, reading, highlighting, creating flash cards of new terms, as well as rereading your notes every day. Practice makes perfect. So, the next question becomes, from a psychological standpoint—how do we learn? What is going on in our brains? The next section will address these questions.

Information-processing Theory

My guess is that most folks have never thought twice about how our brains process information. Psychologically speaking, what is happening within our brains that allows us to remember some bit of information from many years ago when we were six years old, but at the same time, means we may have a very difficult time remembering what Dr. So-and-So was talking about in lecture just the other day? Currently, four theories of information processing are receiving significant attention. For the most part, all the current theories are very similar to each other, varying only in minor details. Below is a schematic diagram of the information-processing theory Atkinson and Shiffrin proposed in the early 1970s.

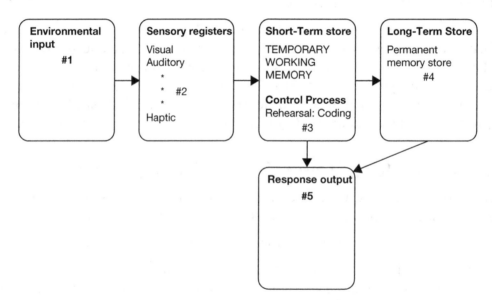

Here Is the Basic Idea of How It All Works

1. ***Environmental input*** is nothing more than the information, whether it's the spoken word or an experience we are encountering at any given point in time. Finding out what happens when we touch a stove burner that is red hot is an example of environmental input.

2. This environmental input is immediately encountered by one of our five senses or ***sensory registers***. Given the above example, the sensory register in question is that of touch.

3. The information experienced by the sensory registers is then sent directly to the ***short-term memory***. Once in the short-term memory, certain ***control processes*** take over, such as rehearsal (which is not the same as memorization), coding, and/or imaging. Coding refers to the control process in which the information to be remembered is contextualized with other similar experiences, such as being burned by a cigarette or a campfire.

4. If the information that is in the short-term memory is processed sufficiently, it will then move to the ***long-term memory***, which is presumed to be limitless in its capacity to hold information.

5. Once information reaches either the short-term or long-term memory, we are then able to make the appropriate ***response output***. If we use the example of touching the hot stove, the appropriate response would be not to touch a hot stove again.

At this point, you may be asking yourself why we need a long-term memory at all. According to the figure shown above, we can give an appropriate response from either the short-term or the long-term memory. So, why do we need both? In the mid-1950s a Harvard researcher, George Miller, conducted research regarding the short-term memory capacity that plays a pivotal role in the current information-processing theories used today. Miller's groundbreaking research has shown that the short-term memory has a limited capacity to hold information gathered via environmental input. The title of his research paper says it all, *"The Magical Number Seven, Plus or Minus Two..."* Hence, the short-term memory is only capable of holding seven, plus or minus two, chunks or bits of information.

Once information has entered the short-term memory bank, one of two things occurs. First, it is purged from the short-term memory; hence, it is forgotten. Second, through various mechanisms such as rehearsal and imagery, information is sent to the long-term memory bank, which is assumed to be limitless in its capacity. Therefore, your goal as a student is to get information that is presented to you via lectures, papers, group work, presentations, and the like into your long-term memory. One way to make this transfer of knowledge occur is, as already mentioned, through the rehearsal of information.

Now you may ask the question, "How do the long-term and short-term memory banks relate to the way I study?" As you can see from the information-processing theory, as well as many other research studies, we learn and therefore store information in our long-term memories through repetition. If your goal is to get new information into your long-term memories, you must rehearse or practice that information. There is a large body of research in existence that shows that "cramming" for exams the night before or two nights before an exam is ineffective in getting information into the long-term memory. Therefore, you need to read your notes and books on a daily basis, every day from the first day of class. If you approach your education in this fashion, three outcomes are likely to occur.

1. You will receive better grades than if you "cram" the night before the exam.
2. You will actually learn the material, allowing you to better serve society and make connections across many disciplines.
3. If numbers one and two occur, then number three becomes a reality; that is getting into graduate school or professional school, or landing the dream job you are looking for.

My Productive Schedule for Success

Once I finally learned some valuable study and time management skills, my junior and senior years of my undergraduate career were very successful, as were both my master's and doctorate careers. I cannot say the same for my first two years of college. The reasoning here is simple—I did not know how to study nor manage my time effectively. Noting that there are many ways to approach your education with success in mind, below is a strategy that I found very helpful in completing my undergraduate as well as my graduate degrees.

- Reading the appropriate chapters prior to going to class
- Highlighting important information after I have read a passage
- Creating flash cards of unfamiliar terms
- Attending class—not just some classes but all classes
- Active listening in class
- Taking notes in class
- Rewriting my notes
- And, finally, reading my notes every day—yes, I said every day!

Allowing information to flow to our long-term memory, which is where we want it to end up eventually, takes practice. This practice in turn has a very positive correlation to performing well on exams and, in turn, your GPA. When we perform well on exams, we then go to graduate school, professional school or enter the career that we have chosen for ourselves. This, my friends is a win-win situation!

Stress and Exams

Taking exams, as we all probably have experienced can be a very stressful time, especially if we are ill prepared for the exam. So, one sure-fire way to help us perform to our greatest potential is by removing, the best we can, stress from the testing equation.

So what? Why is maintaining your stress level of importance in regards to your performance on exams? When we are stressed out, our bodies release norepinephrine, which is responsible for the fight-or-flight response. This response can cause our performance to suffer. Your heart rate increases, blood pressure increases, and you sweat more. Therefore, negative consequences are expressed as anxiousness and irritability, which in part causes us to think less clearly relative to having reduced stress levels. These behaviors may in turn have a negative effect on your test performance. If we follow the aforementioned advice of a proper diet, a good night's sleep, and creating and following a study schedule, our stress level will be reduced greatly when it comes to test time. Eliminating stress completely from our day-to-day activities is unrealistic. Therefore, learning valuable stress-reduction techniques, such as deep breathing and meditation, to keep your stress within manageable limits also will help curtail the stress you may feel at examination time. Your counseling center located on campus will be able to help you manage your stress levels.

Also of importance is the idea us using positive self-talk as opposed to being overly negative, as these are often self-fulfilling prophecies. If you tell yourself you are going to do well on an exam, you will have a much better chance of doing just that, as opposed to telling yourself that, "I am going to flunk this test." If that is what you tell yourself, if that is what you believe, then there is a good chance that this is exactly what is going to happen.

Test-taking Strategies

A great amount of emphasis is placed on your ability to take tests. Whether we like it or not, it's the name of the game in college. Exams will come at you in all sorts of shapes and sizes. The commonality here is that you will probably only have two to four exams in a class for the entire semester. That means that performing well on each of them is of critical importance. So let's discuss some strategies related to the different testing styles that you will no doubt encounter throughout your college experience.

Essay Exams

Essay exams often will highlight one's ability to think critically. There are some strategies you may want to consider.

1. Read all of the essay questions prior to beginning. I would propose that after reading all the questions, you choose the one(s) that you feel most comfortable answering and attend to those first.

2. Budget your time. If you have 60 minutes to finish a six-question exam, you certainly do not want to spend 30 minutes on the first question. So, know where the clock is in the classroom, or make sure that you have a watch to monitor your time.

3. You may want to create an outline for each question and stick to that outline. If you have answered all the questions and have time left, you may then consider revisiting each question to elaborate, if need be.

4. Be concise with your writing. The name of the game here is not to see how wordy you can be (professors can see right through this strategy when grading papers). Rather, you want to answer, completely, the question(s) at hand. As scientists, we write short, sweet, and to the point. As a rule, you will not receive extra points for pontification.

Multiple-choice Exams

Here, as with all test questions, the first thing you will want to do is read the directions closely. Multiple-choice exams typically will want you to circle the correct answer.

That said, some multiple-choice exams will have more than one correct answer. If so, the directions will ask you to circle all the correct answers for each question. Also, it is important to read each and every question with a critical eye. After reading each question, answer it before looking at the possible answers listed below the question.

I would suggest if you run across a question that you do not feel comfortable answering you should leave it alone and return to it later. Often, times reading and answering other multiple-choice exam questions will jog your memory in relation to a question you have left unanswered earlier. Also, if you first answer questions you know the answers to, your stress level will more than likely be reduced. Again, reducing our stress levels is always a good thing for performing well on an exam.

When reading your questions, identify key words such as *all, always, never, none, not, few, many, some, and sometimes.* Next, if you still do not know the answer, you may want to employ the process of elimination for questions about which you are unsure. Often, by crossing out the possible answers that you know are incorrect, you will be left with only one or two possibilities regarding the correct answer. If you still do not know the answer to a question, you may want to focus on the potential answer that is the longest. Certainly, you do not want to pick it blindly because it is the longest. Critically examine the longest because often, a correct answer requires a longer explanation than does an incorrect answer. Read all the choices for each question prior to choosing your answer. You may come to item "b" and say, yep, that is the right answer. If you do this, you would miss the correct answer that says both items "b" and "d" are correct.

True-false Exam Questions

True-false questions typically are formatted to test students' knowledge of specific factual information. Therefore, they are objective because only one answer is correct—it is either true or false. First, as with all test questions, you will want to read them closely. While reading, you will want to look for key words or phrases. You are looking for clues here. Words such as *all, always, never, none, not, few, many, some, and sometimes* will provide very important clues about the validity of the questions on the exam.

Why Be So Concerned with Sleep, Nutrition, Information Processing, Scheduling, and Exam Preparation?

The answer here is very simple and straight forward. You, the student, are about to enter an entirely different world than what you have experienced thus far in your education. Upon entry into this new world, you'll meet new challenges. Over the years, psychological and biological (in part) researchers have amassed a plethora of research showing that academic performance at the university level is highly correlated with how well students adjust to this new world of college. This adjustment will be accompanied with something called self-efficacy and stress, both of which can have a direct impact on your success as a student.

Self-efficacy can be defined as self-evaluation of your abilities to perform well to reach your desired outcomes. Your desired outcomes at this level of education will be expressed as your GPA, as well as your ability to persist from year to year in a highly competitive college environment. If your desired outcomes are reached at the undergraduate level, they will be pleasantly rewarded once you graduate and attend graduate or professional school or obtain the career you have dreamed of for many years. Please note, our jobs as college professors is to challenge you—and challenge you we will!

With the appropriate approach to your college education—by doing most, if not all, of what has been spoken of so far, your self-efficacy will increase, your stress levels will decrease, and your grades will be high. This, my friends, is a win-win situation.

GRADES, GRADES, GRADES!

Students often feel that all anyone wants to know about them is their grades. Parents want to know, advisors want to know, and potential employers or admissions committees to medical school, dental school, law school, or graduate school want to know. Why is there so much emphasis on grades?

Grades, or your grade point average (GPA), tell quite a lot about you as a student and your potential for entering graduate school, professional school, or a career in the biological sciences. Your GPA, in many cases, reflects your overall native intellectual ability, and it certainly says something about your maturity, seriousness of purpose, study habit skills, work ethic, and your ability to stay focused—all attributes that postgraduate schools or employers are seeking. Many potential employers on campus do not want to see students whose GPA is below a certain minimum. Graduate schools generally will not consider students whose GPA is below 3.2. Admission to graduate or professional schools typically requires a much higher GPA, usually in the 3.5 range. Most schools and programs have a GPA minimum, which a student must have in order to be considered at all, and that minimum GPA requirement is usually around a 2.8. These minimums are set for good reason, and that is because we want to be as sure as possible that students will be successful and contributing members at the next level, whether it's graduate or professional school.

Your goal while in college is to succeed to your fullest potential, and if not in Biological Sciences, then in some other academic area where your talents might be more productive.

First, an editorial from *The Roanoke Times*.

College Is a Privilege, Not a Mandate

The Roanoke Times: Commentary
Tonia Moxley, English Instructor at Virginia Tech
Reprinted with permission of *The Roanoke Times*

I have spent the past 10 years of my life at Virginia Tech, first as a student and now a faculty member. In my educational capacity, I work closely with the student population, and I have come to the conclusion that most of the students attending college should never have been admitted to the university.

The students I teach, with some notable exceptions, only sporadically darken the door of the classroom. When they do, they exude an air of profound boredom. Some even claim they feel oppressed. They say they feel burdened by their assignments, and in the equation, I become a taskmaster paid to torment them. Their response to learning is one of suffering as if they have been sentenced to menial labor when they're asked to write a research paper or read an intelligent essay.

In this age of "free thinking," students are free to question or demean the classroom materials chosen by instructors and professors. I particularly enjoy the opinions of 18-year-olds who think that Plato's "Myth of the Cave" is a "bunch of crap." Perhaps students need to learn how to think under supervision before they are allowed to attempt it on their own.

Then, there are some who think the university is out to indoctrinate them. They claim that someone from Admissions kidnapped them, forcing them to spend their parents' money on an education. There are a few who do not want to learn how to use commas properly because it squashes their "creative expression."

When I was an undergraduate, I had a semester of rebellion. I skipped class too much. I partied too much. I paid the consequences. But never in any of that time did I lose sight of the fact that it was a privilege to be here—an expensive one. I also knew I had made my own choices.

In ten years, a myth seems to have sprung up among students. They seem to think that a college education is a compulsory extension of high school. Perhaps some of the responsibility could be laid at the door of the university administration. Money is much on the minds of all the powers that be these days, and out-of-state tuition seems to be too much of a temptation to resist–no matter how low the test scores.

We can also blame the state government. After all, our governor wants high school kids to be able to bring high-powered hunting rifles to school. Imagine what he wants kids to bring to college.

But I can't change my nature. I cannot believe that the university administration and the state government bear all the responsibility for apathetic, undereducated students who treat higher education as a matter of course:

College is not compulsory. It's a hard-earned privilege.

WHAT DO FORMER UNDERGRADUATES HAVE TO SAY ABOUT THEIR COLLEGE EXPERIENCE?

I have had the pleasure of working with literally thousands of students during my time as a college professor. Some have been very successful and some not so much. I often try to communicate to my incoming students some of the trials and tribulations that my students and I have experienced over time. I feel that sometimes when I try to pass this information along, some undergraduates tend to think that what I tell them is unrealistic and is more of a view from a professor's viewpoint. Therefore, I asked a few of my successful undergraduates the following questions so you can hear it straight from the "horse's mouth" so to speak. Here is what they had to say.

Question No. 1

What were the most important differences you encountered between your high school experience and your undergraduate experience?

Philip Ruffner said, "Probably the most significant difference between high school and undergrad was the size of lectures. In undergrad, I was just another face in the crowd. That is, until I introduced myself to my professors and started to develop a relationship with them. Professors in undergrad are certainly eager to assist and help in any way possible, but the babysitting is over. You are responsible for your own work and must have the desire and work ethic to be a successful college student, with that, you will see great rewards."

Tim Wicks responded, "The most important and biggest difference between high school and undergrad was freedom (both good and bad). The good: I lived on my own time; I was able to develop my own time management skills and get things done when and the way I wanted to. The bad: I had to quickly learn the meaning of "accountability." I now realize that there was a reason for my parents' pressure and rules for me to always complete my high school work before doing something for leisure. It is exponentially more difficult to play catch up in undergrad than in high school."

Ren Harman believes: "High school has been said to be a foundation of what makes a person who they are, whereas in college you are adding to that foundation to make a permanent structure. Personally for me, everything changed once I started college. New friends, new subjects, new everything and although that may not work for everyone, it was exactly what I needed. You learn so much in four years in college, about who you are as a person and develop opinions, beliefs, and values that can never be learned through the system of high school. Differences between the two range far and wide, from class size to friend size, from differences in teachers and professors, and what exactly you are supposed to study for the test, it will all change. The undergraduate experience is quite different from the high school experience, regardless of where you are from and who you are, but in the end, a better person will arise."

Question No. 2

What were the most important differences that you experienced between your high school teachers and your college professors during your undergraduate experience?

Philip Ruffner said, "High school teachers were just that, teachers. At Virginia Tech, the professors that I encountered were more than teachers or educators. Throughout my college career, professors at VT became colleagues, mentors, counselors, and friends. High school teachers served as training wheels on a bike; they helped to guide you through the hallways without tipping over. Undergrad professors helped you, the bike rider, to go faster, to be more confident, and to handle the power, freedom, and responsibility of riding a bike."

Tim Wicks responded, "In terms of high school teacher and college professors, I feel that both cared for the well-being of the student equally. However, the vast majority of my college professors had their doctorates in their respective fields (compared to three high school teachers with doctorates). They were far more knowledgeable on the subject matter. That is not to say, however, that my high school teachers did not know anything and were horrible teachers. It was absolutely to the contrary, in fact. It goes without saying, though, that a faculty of mostly doctorates, many of whom are currently involved in research, provide a wonderful opportunity to learn from, interact with and work with experts who are absolute authorities in their respective fields."

Ren Harman proposes, "Building relationships with your college professors is one of the most important things you should do during your undergraduate education. Unlike in high school, college professors do not know your parents or siblings that they may have taught, or maybe where you even live, they are complete strangers. From the first day of class, until the day you receive your diploma, creating and maintain a relationship with your professors is highly crucial in your success during your undergraduate education, as well as post graduation. College professors have hundreds and possibly thousands of students, not to mention their research and outside involvement with the university. Making yourself known and feeling comfortable around all of your professors will pay greatly in the end. Get to know them, visit them during their office hours, and attend study sessions. Building a relationship with your professors will lead to research and teaching assistant positions, letters of recommendation, and a multitude of other opportunities, whereas you may never think about a high school teacher again.

Question No. 3

What were the major adjustments you had to make coming from high school to college?

Philip Ruffner said, "The biggest adjustment I had to make in the transition from high school to undergrad was self-accountability. I quickly found that it was up to me to become a successful college student. With the new found freedom of being so far from home, it was challenging to stay focused."

Tim Wicks responded with, "I had to make two major adjustments (and very quickly) during my first year of undergrad. 1) As previously stated, I had to develop my own time management skills. I had no one checking up on me to make sure I got all of my assignments completed on time. Basically, I learned how to become accountable for my own actions/failures. 2) I had to learn *how* to study.

Even in all honors and advanced-level classes in high school, I was never challenged enough to actually need to study for exams. I was able to retain enough information, basically from just showing up to class and listening to receive all A's. However, this method does *not* apply to undergrad courses.

Both biology and chemistry lectures move so much faster and throw so much more information at you, it is impossible to just show up and take it all in. Learning the importance of and learning how to study is crucial. Everyone has their own way that works for them, but it is imperative that you figure out what works best for you and, going back to number one, do *not* get behind. Start early, and study often. Otherwise, you will be sorely disappointed with your first semester GPA, just as I was.

Ren Harman states, "Coming from a small high school graduating class to a rather large university such as Virginia Tech, the list of major adjustments that I personally had to make is quite a lengthy list, but here are a few of the highlights.

1. Read, read, read your textbooks; a majority of questions in your mind can be answered by simply reading the required text before coming to class. It seems like such a simple task, but it is a trap that I have seen every college student waltz right into. Reading the text and preparing before lecture will make studying for the quiz/exam/final or whatever it may be a much simpler task.

2. Find what works for you when preparing for tests and exams, whether studying alone, studying in a group or maybe a little bit of both, if you have a question about the material, chances are someone else in your group has the exact same question, and someone else in that same group will probably have the answer.

3. Stay hungry and stay passionate about what you are learning; high school at times can be so bland, but in college, you are really learning a career and so so many life lessons along the way.

Summing It Up

I could not have said it better myself. The above passages come straight from the horse's mouth so to speak; these students were all successful undergraduates who are currently enrolled in professional and graduate schools. Hopefully, the above responses have highlighted some of the major differences that my former students have encountered while making the transition from high school and entering the very different world of higher education. While the above responses are only voiced from three former students of mine, they are very typical of what I (and my colleagues) hear from most of our former students and are packed with some very powerful information.

Work ethic and accountability are two very important tools that all successful college students must have. At the beginning of each semester, you the student will be given a syllabus for each of your classes. You now have a road map of sorts as to exactly what the professor expects, and when, throughout the semester. Gone are the days of high school where your teacher told you every day what was expected of you, made sure that you had completed your homework, or reminded you that a test was coming up and you should be studying for it. Higher education is different. You have been given the syllabus for the semester, and you will need to respond accordingly. We as professors are always here to help, but we will not chase you down to make sure you have done your reading or homework. It is up to you!

As Mr. Ruffner (soon to be Dr. Ruffner) points out in question number two, "High school teachers served as training wheels on a bike ... they helped to guide you through the hallways without tipping over. Undergrad professors helped you, the bike rider, to go faster, to be more confident, and to handle the power, freedom, and responsibility of riding a bike." Further, Dr. Wicks acknowledges that most of us (faculty) have our doctorates and, therefore, we are experts in our chosen fields of study. For these reasons, among others, it is very important to meet and get to know you professors because they do in fact hold the answers and can help guide you to the next level. That said, they can only guide you if you get to know them. Again, it is up to you. If you follow their advice, as well as mine, you will have a much greater opportunity to realize your dreams and potential.

So, who are these three people? Phillip Ruffner is a graduate of Virginia Tech with a Bachelor of Science degree in the Biological Sciences. He is currently in his third year of dental school at Virginia Commonwealth University. Tim Wicks also graduated from Virginia Tech with a Bachelor of Science degree in Human Nutrition Foods and Exercise and has just completed his doctorate degree in physical therapy. Ren Harman received his Bachelor of Science degree in the Biological Sciences and is currently a graduate student pursuing his PhD in Edcational Psychology.

They were all advisees of mine, they all took the time to get to know me as well as many of their other professors, and they were all teaching assistants for me. They performed exceptionally as undergraduates, they took ownership of their education, and they found the necessary time and effort to meet professors; I wrote letters of recommendation for each of them for their respective graduate and or professional schools. They are all perfect examples of the success you can have as undergraduates. They all had, and still do have, tremendous work ethics and the accountability necessary to excel in higher education.

Which Way to Go? Pathways to Help Achieve Your Goals—Options

Regardless of your undergraduate institution, your Department of Biological Sciences will probably have several areas of specialization to help majors focus on specific career pathways. These areas, often called options or Tracks, simply provide a series of courses within the major that help students point their "compass" in a specific direction. Completion of a specific option is typically noted on the university's official transcript, but not on the diploma. If specific options or tracks are not available to you at your chosen institution, there are typically a broad selective of science electives available. You will be able to create, to a degree, your own personalized curriculum.

In some cases, if you are extremely competitive, the senior year may be spent in the first year of residency in a postgraduate professional school (medical, dental school, nursing, veterinary medicine, or pharmacy school). You can then transfer course credits completed in the first year of residency which may then be transferred back to your undergraduate institution to complete biology elective and free elective requirements for the completion of your undergraduate degree. As a rule all required course work must be completed prior to your first year of professional school. For example, all curriculum for liberal education requirements must be satisfied, as well as all mandatory biology, chemistry, physics, math, and statistics courses must be completed prior to enrolling in a professional program. Therefore, only biology elective hours should remain unfulfilled at the time of appointment to a professional program.

Some options/tracks almost guarantee employment immediately upon graduation (Food Science and Technology, Clinical Laboratory Science, and Biotechnology), while others are stepping-stones to graduate and professional schools. If one or more of these interest you, consult with your advisor, who will be able to answer your questions and concerns.

Options and Tracks for Biological Sciences Majors

Science departments typically will offer seven formal or informal options/tracks regarding your sub-discipline within biology. These are designated tracks designed to help students focus on specific curricula. Detailed information and check sheets for options related to your degree can be found on your departmental website, the department advising office, or with your advisor. Therefore, if you have a particular interest within the field of biology, it will be important to check with the appropriate authorities to see exactly what your options are. Below is a list of potential options that may be of interest to you.

Microbiology/Immunology Option

The Microbiology/Immunology Option may be available to students interested in pursuing a career in Microbiology and or Immunology. The course of study typically is very similar to the regular BS degree in Biological Sciences. With that said, students enrolled in this option concentrate their biology electives in microbiology and related courses. The Microbiology/Immunology Option allows students to prepare for advanced degrees in Microbiology and Immunology or for direct entry into the workforce without additional training.

Biotechnology Track

The option in Biotechnology is an interdisciplinary and interdepartmental program that draws upon the expertise of several departments such as the College of Agriculture and Life Sciences, the College of Science, and the College of Engineering. Majors from participating departments in these three colleges may add this option to the BS degree. Students who complete the BS degree in Biology with the option in Biotechnology will find numerous opportunities for employment as laboratory scientists with many expanding biotechnology and pharmaceutical firms in the area and nationwide. Completion of the Biotechnology option, supplemented by additional courses in chemistry and advanced biology, is also an excellent way to prepare for graduate school in areas of biology that utilize genetics and molecular biology to answer a broad variety of experimental questions.

Pre-Med, Pre-Dent, Pre-Pharmacy, and Pre-Vet Track

It is very typical that entering freshmen from year to year are enrolled, either officially or unofficially, in one of these tracks. It is not unusual for at least 60 percent of the incoming freshmen in biology to be enrolled in one of these tracks. These options are typically created by the university in question to ensure that all students will complete the necessary prerequisites needed to enter one of these professional schools.

Bio-Business Track

Completion of the Bio-Business track will provide students with a general background in business that is required by many biologically based companies. Biology and the biosciences are no longer relegated to research labs in universities, government, or with pharmaceutical companies. A bio-business industry has developed and is one of the leading areas of economic growth throughout the world. Not only Bio-Business companies need students trained in biotechnology techniques, but also firms need students with training in both the sciences and business. Students who wish more depth, or who may eventually enter an MBA program, may want to consider the minor in Business.

Food Science and Technology Track

Food science and Technology is the application of science and technology to the processing, preservation, packaging, distribution, and utilization of foods and food products. Students who complete this track will gain an understanding of the nature, properties, and characteristics of foods as determined through biochemistry, chemistry, microbiology, physics, and other sciences. Food scientists extend this knowledge to the development of new products, processes, equipment, and packages; to the selection of proper raw products and ingredients; and to the adequate direction of plant operations so that processed foods high in nutritive value and quality are produced economically.

Food science and technology is the key to the conversion of raw agricultural materials into a wide variety of properly processed and preserved foods, thus providing an important contribution to the well-being, economy, standard of living, and progress of humanity. Students who complete the track in Food Science and Technology will find employment opportunities in the food industry in research and development, manufacturing and production, technical sales and service, management, quality control, inspection services with state or federal government, technical writing, teaching, and consulting work. Students in this track will work closely with faculty in Food Science and Technology to develop resumes and meet potential employers.

Ecology Track

The Ecology Track is designed for students working toward a BS degree in Biological Sciences who want to emphasize ecology in their course selection. Because most careers in ecology require training beyond the BS degree, this track is designed to provide background for further study and training so that students completing this track will be competitive in their applications for postgraduate study. However, it also will provide a general ecological awareness that will be useful in various other careers for students entering the job market immediately upon graduation.

Making the Most of It

"Scirene Vultis?" Summer 1996 Vol. VII Number 1
Dr. Charles J Dudley
Reprinted with permission of author

Most students go to college—which is a mistake. Students who excel *do* college—which means they gain all that is possible from the experience. If you wish to make the most of college, come prepared to do. Do what? You might ask. The answer is easy: plan to study as you have never studied in your life. The opportunity given you will not last long and the record that you compile will mark you forever. Let me explain.

College is about you and what you wish to do with your life. I say this with great care. The focus is on you and what you do. You are beginning your adult life and are privileged enough to start with several years of additional preparation. How valuable they are to you depends entirely on how you approach your education and how hard you are willing to work. Based on years of observing students graduate, I offer the following advice: Regardless of all else, place academics first.

Many wonderful things happen to a person in the course of a college education—many of them have little to do with academics. New friends, close relationships, new clubs and other organizations, and being totally on your own only begin to list the possibilities. Let's face it, the college environment is exciting—and fun. More significantly, all of these things are important parts of life and should not be ignored. However, the central reason for college is study. Study is the first thing to do—it is doing college.

A few more years from now there will be an accounting of your efforts. When you graduate, employers, graduate schools, professional schools, and other interested parties seek virtually no data on how much fun you had in college. Nor will they ask how many friends you made, or close relationships you enjoyed. They will want to know your grade-point average, whether or not you did undergraduate research, how many faculty you got to know well professionally, what positions of responsibility you held, the development of your leadership skills, and your potential ability to get things done, make things happen. For those who do college, the answers to their questions will yield wonderful results; for those who went to college, things will be good, but there will always be the nagging thoughts about "if only I had."

Students in the University Honors Program, and others, tell me that I sometimes intimidate students (particularly first-year students) when I discuss the significance of college. Strangely enough, I agree with them. For those of you beginning college this fall, you begin the development of your life's work on an adult level. The record of accomplishment you begin this year provides the foundation for all you might wish for yourself in the future. Measure yourself carefully and arrive here in the fall with your goals intact, your plans made, and ready to go to work. This is a great university; make the most of it.

Undergraduate Research: A Capstone Experience

Aside from grades, you will need to have one or more professors at the university who can write letters of recommendation on your behalf for employment or admission to postgraduate schools. There is no way that a letter of quality can be written unless the professor knows you reasonably well. As spoken of earlier, one professor who could write such a letter, if you have taken the initiative to develop a professional relationship, is your advisor. The other person could be your research mentor.

Letters of recommendation need to talk about you as a person. All the things that your parents, grandparents, aunts, and uncles have said were important about character now become important, and someone must be able to write about them. These issues may include, but are not limited to, issues such as: work ethic, punctuality, honesty, sincerity, and ability to work alone or in groups, ability to follow directions, aptitude for learning, communication skills and ability, in writing as well as in the spoken word.

One of the best ways to gauge your ability for research and to develop a professional relationship with a mentor is through an undergraduate research program.

As you enter your sophomore or junior year, you should be laying plans for this activity. In some cases, students choose to volunteer to work in one or more laboratories before approaching a professor about undergraduate research. In other cases, professors will not consider taking a student into their lab until they have had the student in class and can gauge their academic ability and seriousness. In other instances, inroads to undergraduate research can potentially be made through your graduate teaching assistants in a laboratory course. In any case, the opportunity to become involved depends upon your initiative, as a professor is not going to actively search for you to become a member of their research team. Again, it is up to *you*!

Also bear in mind that biology is practiced in many departments across campus other than the Department of Biological Sciences, and these other departments are fertile grounds for undergraduate research opportunities. For example, my students often will undertake undergraduate research with the Departments of Chemistry, Biochemistry, Human Nutrition Foods and Exercise, Entomology, or Plant Pathology Physiology and Weed Science, just to name a few. By going through the websites of these departments, including the Department of Biological Sciences, students have the ability to review the faculty members and their respective fields of research; find a field of interest; see what prerequisites a given faculty member may have for undergraduate research: and find their office location, laboratory, and email address. All that is left is taking the initiative to make contact.

How Do Today's College Graduates Stack Up against the Skill Needed to Be Successful in the Twenty-first-century Workforce?

The following information, from the National Center for Higher Education Management Systems (NCHEMS), synthesizes their recent research, including interviews with thousands of employers, which revealed the knowledge, skills, and attitudes necessary for success in the twenty-first-century workforce. This issue compares what many undergraduates learn in college, and the knowledge and skills necessary to be successful in today's workforce.

NCHEMS identifies four categories of knowledge, skills, and attitude necessary for success in the twenty-first-century workforce:

1. Attitude and personal characteristics (e.g., adaptability, reliability, professionalism, punctuality)
2. Essential skills for entry-level employment (e.g., computer skills, which are "essential skills" applied to more complex situations, as well as communication skills)
3. Integrative-applied skills, which are "essential skills," applied in more complex situations (e.g., critical thinking, presentation skills)
4. Premium skills, which are not mandatory, but are important additions to "essential" and integrative-applied skills (e.g., ethics, multicultural competence skills)

Throughout their discussions with employers, NCHEMS discovered that a gap exists between what many undergraduates learn in college and the knowledge and skills necessary to succeed in the twenty-first-century workforce. Employers indicate that **many recent graduates:**

- **Cannot communicate effectively orally or in writing**
- **Cannot solve real world "messy" problems**
- **Have difficulty working in teams**

What does this gap mean for post-secondary curricula, and therefore you?

- Students need to write more.
- Students need to learn how to write in different contexts, not just how to phrase perfect sentences.
- Students need exposure to, and experience with, not only solving, but also with identifying real-world "messy" problems that defy neat definitions.

An excellent educational opportunity has been offered to you here at your chosen institution. Your college or univesity likely has some of the best and brightest researchers in the world. If you, the student, choose to take advantage of all that surrounds you here, you will become the best of the best. When you do, many doors will swing wide open for you, whether you find that perfect job you have dreamed about for years or are accepted to a professional or graduate program. But, remember, at the end of the day, *it is all up to you!*

Co-Op Programs, Internship Programs, Externship Programs, Field-study Experience, and Undergraduate Research

Students who wish to find employment immediately upon graduation are often caught on the horns of a dilemma: "it's hard to find a job if you haven't had a job" or "how do I make myself competitive if I don't have work experience?" The bottom line is that, if you wish to find employment or acceptance to a professional or graduate school immediately upon graduation and you have to be competitive, you must be as attractive as you can be. Life after college is very competitive! You need to use your undergraduate years to build a resume that shows work experience. I would suggest you read the following article by Dr. Camille Wright Miller: entitled "Students Need the Experience of Internships."

There are a multitude of avenues in which students can gain relevant work experience while an undergraduate in the Department of Biological Sciences at their chosen institution. These are through the Cooperative Education program (Co-op), Field Study, Undergraduate Research, Internships, Externships, or summer employment in the world of science. Having some experience prior to applying for whatever is next after your undergraduate career is of the utmost importance.

I say this because everyone you will be competing against for a position in the work force or graduate or professional school will have more than likely, excellent credentials. So the question becomes, what makes you more attractive than, potentially, the hundreds or thousands of people with whom you are competing? The answer to this question may very well be *experience*. If you have experience, you will become much more attractive than those who do not.

Benefits to You, the Student

The avenues listed above provide an opportunity for students to gain real-life work experience. Interaction with professional people gives them the opportunity to write letters of recommendation about your personality, character, and work ethic. Without these letters of reference about you, it is extremely difficult to find a position after graduation in a competitive environment. Take the initiative to meet faculty, gain their confidence, and create an opportunity to gain valuable work experience. The benefits at graduation time will be well worth the effort.

Cooperative Education (Co-Op)

Cooperative Education is normally a five-year educational program that is designed to enhance academic knowledge, personal development, and preparation for a professional career. By blending the traditional academic function of the university with work assignments in industry, business, government, and community services, the program affords students the opportunity to integrate academic training and practical work experience. The Co-op program allows students who are at the sophomore and/or junior level to alternate school semesters with Co-op semesters, utilizing the entire calendar year, and thus accumulate from 12 to 18 months of work experience prior to graduation. This acquisition of pre-professional experience presents the Co-op student with the opportunity to test career goals, defray the costs of a college education, and gain the all-important edge in the permanent employment market. Often, Co-ops have specific requirements that all students must meet prior to acceptance. For more information, visit the career center on your campus.

Internships

One of the more popular avenues of gaining work experience is through Internships. Normally, Internships do not pay a summer wage, and in many cases, the student must pay for the experience. An example of the latter situation would be an opportunity to work at a shark or dolphin research lab for the summer. Students would have to pay a nominal fee for the opportunity to be involved in such research, and the selection process would be on a competitive basis. Your department typically will offer academic credit for science-based internships through courses such as Field Study. Students interested in acquiring college credit for the internship experiences should contact their department prior to undertaking an internship.

"Students Need the Experience of Internships"
Camille Wright Miller
Reprinted with permission of *The Roanoke Times*

Over the last several weeks, I've been working with a group of college students who will graduate this Spring. I was invited to meet with them to discuss the interviewing and hiring process. I talked with them about the protocol of interviewing, about "presentation of self" and all other areas related to interviewing successfully. I told them what the process looks like from the employer's side.

At the conclusion of the meeting, I offered to review their resumes and give feedback on how well their considerable thought had gone into the writing of the resumes. For the most part, the resumes were correctly formatted. They had been proofread for typographical errors. I made only minor suggestions for improvement.

Unfortunately, only minor suggestions could be made. It is too late in the process for these seniors to correct the most glaring weakness that emerged from the review of the resumes. For most of them, the glaring weakness is the lack of experience. Their extracurricular activities are strong. For most, their grade point average demonstrates solid academic work. Too few, though, had sufficient experience in the work world—a critical element in setting oneself above other candidates.

I don't announce that unsympathetically. I remember my first job search. I remember the frustration of "you don't have experience." I remember the unending circularity of the problem: I couldn't get hired without experience; I couldn't gain experience without being hired.

The difference between then and now is that students can and should gain experience while still in college. Internships add power to the graduating student's resume. Internships provide evidence that a student is exploring the work world, exploring careers, has put some thought into specific career areas and, most important, has some experience.

The subject of internships makes me think of other students who have graduated and are enjoying successful careers. I've known students who experienced internships in federal and state offices, in local governments, in publishing, and in business. These were students who had new internships the summers of their rising sophomore, junior, and senior years. Each student grew from the experiences. Each identified specific areas to pursue and specific areas to be avoided.

Finding internships is not extremely difficult. Each college career development center has a listing of internships that are offered to that college. Students who are unsure about what they want to do can scan the opportunities for ones that appear interesting. For those students who are focused, the career development center, in partnership with the alumni office, can identify graduates who are employed in a particular field. Students can write and call those alumni, ask for some insider guidance, and propose internships.

As a side note to those considering internships, project internships are the most productive. In these situations, a particular project is given to the intern—creating a new database, creating a Web site, or implementing and summarizing a survey. Project internships provide students a product to highlight on their resumes.

I am sorry that the students I'm working with are in their last semester. They are smart, talented, and well educated. But they have serious gaps on their resumes. They need experience. Think how different those resumes would look had they taken advantage of what has become, at some schools, an expectation.

Undergraduate Research in Biological Sciences

Most faculty members in the sciences are involved in the discovery of new knowledge, as well as in conveying known knowledge (teaching). This is arrangement is consistent with what is expected at all major universities. Much of the reputation of a department and institution is judged by national and international peers on the quality of these new discoveries. In the graduate experience, teaching and research comes together in training students who receive MS and PhD degrees. Over the past few years, many faculty also have provided selected undergraduate students opportunities to "put knowledge to work" in their research laboratories. Faculty in universities enjoy working with undergraduate students, but you should be aware that research projects require use of facilities, equipment, supplies, and time. While most of these resources are committed to graduate student training for advanced degrees, several faculty find the time, space, and funds to work with undergraduate students on appropriate research projects. Sometimes, students will work with a graduate student in the research lab.

Since lab space and time are somewhat limited, undergraduate research cannot be offered to all students. Researchers often only accept undergraduates who have excelled academically. Research cannot always be packaged in a short time period. A particular laboratory experiment or field observation may require extra time, including some evenings or weekend work. The professor with whom you work will determine the nature of the research project, amount of academic credit, work expectations, and final evaluation of your research. Undergraduate research can be done at any time during your undergraduate career. That said, students typically will become involved in undergraduate research during their sophomore or junior years. Depending on when you begin, you could have multiple semesters of research experience upon graduation.

Undergraduate Research is the process by which students work in a professor's lab and receive academic credit for the experience. This course is typically a variable credit enrollment class, usually for one to four hours' credit. With that said, Undergraduate Research is not a typical class because students will be doing research alongside their professor. To participate, students need to discuss their interest in research with a professor who is currently conducting research in that, or a closely related, area.

Students typically will need to complete an application in advance of the semester in which the research will be conducted, depending on the institution. Many professors are reluctant to provide an undergraduate with a research opportunity until they feel they know the student. Again, we see the importance of getting to know your faculty. This degree of familiarization may be acquired through class work or through the student's volunteering in the professor's lab. Students may contact professors directly and individually in regard to securing a position as an Undergraduate Researcher.

When a student is deemed qualified to participate in the undergraduate research program, this experience will be a significant factor in the career development of young scientists. It provides students with hands-on experience related to research design, experimental techniques, data analysis, scientific literature, and technical writing. Students work closely with a faculty sponsor who directs their research. The diversity of faculty research interests provides students with a wide variety of potential research topics.

Undergraduate research is highly recommended for students who plan a career in graduate school, human medicine, or veterinary medicine. Participation not only exposes students to the methodology of research, but also, it serves as an important factor for acceptance into professional and graduate programs. Research advisors make excellent references for postgraduate work, because of the close working relationship with the students. Students with a particular interest should consult faculty with research expertise in that area to serve as faculty sponsors.

Honors Programs

When competing for postgraduate opportunities, students need to find ways to make their dossier sparkle or standout. One way to accomplish this goal is to distinguish yourself, which can be done, in part, through the Honors Program at your chosen institution. Typically, a college honors program will provide the highly motivated student with an opportunity to work closely with professors, as well as other motivated students, in advanced levels of critical thinking, analysis, research, writing, communication, etc. While honors programs may vary from college to college, the following is a typical summary of some of the procedures and benefits of a college honors program.

Criteria for Entrance

Each honors program potentially will have its own specific entrance requirements. Below is a typical summary of the credential that students admitted to an honors program will need:

- High GPA (usually 3.5 or higher)
- High college admission test scores (usually a combined score of 1,200 or higher on the SAT and/or 26 or higher on the ACT)
- Strong high school curriculum, such as AP, IB, dual enrollment courses
- Top five or ten percent of high school graduation class
- Strong letters of recommendation
- Completion of an entry essay
- Interview with the honors acceptance committee

Please keep in mind that the list above contains examples of some of the many criteria colleges may consider for admittance into an honors program. Criteria will differ from institution to institution. Check with the college's coordinator of the honors program to find out the specific entrance requirements.

How to Apply

For many schools, if you meet their entrance requirements for the honors program, you will be accepted into the program as an incoming freshman upon communication with the honors program of course. Also, if you do not meet the criteria for acceptance as an incoming freshman, worthy students may be asked to join following the successful completion of their freshmen year in college.

While the honors program is not for everyone, there are many associated benefits related to joining the honors program. Below is a list of the possible benefits.

- **Small classes**. Honors courses tend to have a small class size. This in turn allows students a greater opportunity to build strong relationships with the faculty teaching the course. With that said, we have already discussed the great importance of building relationships at the college level.

- **Graduate school preparation**. Most courses taught in honors programs are typically similar in format to graduate school courses, thereby giving participants a foot up, so to speak, when entering graduate school.

- **Special activities**. Students who participate in an honors program often required to contribute at a much deeper level, again similar to what is seen in a graduate program. For instance, honors students typically will complete a thesis prior to their graduation.

- **Scholarship opportunities**. Typically, students participating in an honors program will qualify for certain scholarships that are not available to non-honors students.

- **Priority registration**. Most schools give priority scheduling to students enrolled in the honors program. This is a very valuable tool when it comes to scheduling each semester as an undergraduate.

Major Homework Assignments for College Survival and Life There After

Letter to Advisor, Academic Plan, Career Plan, and Resume

The exercises contained herein are designed to help you the student begin preparing for your career in the Biological Sciences, and as such, they are important for your life after completing your undergraduate degree in the sciences. Each exercise has a theme and examples to help with your approach to creating them. It will be to your advantage to put some energy and time commitment into these exercises and work to complete them to the best of your ability. If you give these assignments your full attention, you will be better able to navigate your undergraduate career, which in turn will allow you the opportunity to excel once you finish your undergraduate career.

What Do I Want to Do with the Rest of My Life?

Your Career Plan

The purpose of this exercise is to provide an opportunity for you to think about what you want to do with your life and a degree in the Biological Sciences. This is not a novel question, and most of us ask the same question throughout our lives. I have colleagues who are planning their retirement after 30 to 35 years of being a university professor, and they are asking the same question!

The point is that you need to know how to articulate your ideas and use resources that will help you to focus on your plan. In general, I advise students to think about what they like to do and evaluate whether they are good at that thing: can you be competitive in your current major at the undergraduate level and perhaps beyond?

Can you be competitive at the next level, considering that you will have to get up and go do it for the rest of your working life (unless of course you change careers)? Can you earn enough money at this occupation to make a living (and in some cases, support yourself and a family)? Is there opportunity for continued professional growth? And lastly, and of critical importance, are you passionate about your career plan?

While an avocation (for instance fishing) sometimes can be turned into a career (retail outlet for fishing equipment and guide service), in many cases, it is wise to keep one's avocational interests somewhat separate from professional interests so that the avocation can be an opportunity to escape the working world.

An actual example is provided for you, in addition to a list of careers most commonly mentioned by freshman biological sciences majors and websites. Furthermore, career services at your institution will provide excellent seminars about career choices and goals.

Your Letter to Your Advisor

This exercise is fairly straightforward. You are to compose a letter introducing yourself to your Freshman Advisor. All students are assigned an Academic Advisor. If you do not know who your advisor is, you should find out immediately. I say this because your advisors should all be schooled in the universities curriculum, as well as its policies and procedures, things about which you the student may not be fully aware. The contents of your paper should include, but are not limited to, telling your advisor a little about yourself. For example, why are you here at the university? What do you want to do with your life, and why? This is an important document, as your advisor will be given a copy of it to read. Thus, it serves as a preamble to the potential relationship that you will have the opportunity to build with your advisor. It will give your advisor some insight about who you are, as well as to show your ability to communicate on a professional level, which is very important at the university level.

Grading

Again, the grading of this paper is straightforward. It will not be graded for content, but rather on your ability to create a professional well-written document.

- 100 points possible. **Each typographical error** will result in a **five (5) point deduction**.

- **Each grammatical error**, such as fragments and run-on sentences, will result in a **five (5) point reduction**.

- The document should be double spaced, 12-point font, and limited to *one* page.

Sometimes students feel my grading scale is much too harsh. Please be aware that my goal, as well as the other professors that you will encounter at your chosen university, is not to see the student perform poorly. Our goal should be the same as yours, and that is to produce the best students possible. At this point in your career, you are aspiring biologists, and many of you are wishing to become physicians, enter graduate school, or enter the professional world directly after graduation. Therefore, we must strive for perfection. With that said, biologists and physicians are required to be accurate and precise all the time—not just sometimes when it suits, but *all the time*. So, we start the journey to perfection today.

Choosing a Career Path

Please answer all *the questions below. Use and document at least four references (i.e., references are needed).*

1. Describe in a paragraph or so something about the activities in a general day for someone involved in the career you plan to research, that is, what will be expected of you on a day-to-day basis. What is the big picture regarding the responsibility for someone in this position?
2. Are there specific courses required from you as an undergraduate to enter your chosen career path? If so, what are they? What education level is needed for your career?
3. Are there specific qualifying exams, such as the Medical College Aptitude Test (MCAT) or the Graduate Record Exam (GRE's)? If so, when should these exams be taken? What is the score one needs on these tests to be competitive at the next level?
4. Is some evidence of needing prior experience required in your chosen career path? If so, what is it, and how much time should be accrued?
5. What is a competitive grade-point average to enter this field?
6. What is the entry-level salary range to be expected?
7. What are the prospects for professional and salary advancement?
8. When should one apply (if needed) to graduate school/professional school to obtain your career goal?
9. Is state residency a factor in competition for your position or seat in a graduate or professional program?
10. What is the employment outlook for the career you have chosen?
11. List all the major sources used to gather information and to indicate where one should go for additional information; in other words, you will need a reference page.

    ➤ *Assignment is to be double-spaced, 12-point font with one-inch margins and in paragraph form.*
    ➤ *Follow APA format.*
    ➤ *Include a title page.*
    ➤ *Include a reference page.*
    ➤ *Wikipedia is not a valid source—Do Not Reference Wikipedia!*

Grading scale

QUESTIONS (1 – 10)

0   1   2   3   4   5   6   7   8

0 = not answered

4 = moderately answered

8 = completely answered

Total possible points = 88

TITLE PAGE (APA format)

0 = none

2 = present

Total possible points = 2

INTEXT REFERENCES

0 = none

1 = present but does not follow requested APA format

2 = well done

Total possible points = 2

AT LEAST FOUR REFERENCES

Fewer than 4 = 0

At least 4 = 4

Total possible points = 4

REFERENCE PAGE

None = 0

Present but does not conform to APA = 2

Follows suggested APA format = 4

Total possible points = 4

TOTAL POINTS POSSIBLE = 100

—5 per typo, not using double spacing, incorrect information, and generally, not following directions.

What Is the Value of Your Research References?

First, and foremost it must be known that your communication skills, both in writing and orally, probably are the most important qualities that each of us will need when we enter graduate or professional school or the workforce. It is of utmost importance to realize that, when we are communicating via the written word, not all references are created equally. Said another way, just because it is written does not mean it is true and or valid. This is especially true when we look at resources found online.

Anyone can create and publish a website. Therefore, you will likely encounter many websites that are not credible and or lack accuracy in regards to your research topic. For example, let's say that you are researching the profession of a pharmacist. *People* magazine (online) may have an article regarding the income and credentials of a pharmacist. On the other hand, there is also an article regarding the income and credentials of a pharmacist on the *American Association of Colleges of Pharmacy (AACP)* website. The AACP will be a much more credible reference than will *People* magazine (online). Conversely, if you wish to know who the best and worst dressed were at the Grammy Awards, then *People* magazine would be your reference given your two choices.

Given the large quantity of potential reference sources found online, it will be important to check several different sources in regards to the same information. Again, let's say we are trying to find the average income for pharmacists. It is always a good idea to check more than one source. For example, if one source tells you the average yearly income for pharmacists is $50,000 per year and another tells you that it is closer to $100,000 per year. That should raise a red flag to you and require you to dig a little deeper and check out other sources as well until you find credible sources that are in agreement with each other.

When you are trying to quantify the quality, reliability, and credibility of your online sources, you may want to look for the following:

- Author's name and or title (is it reputable)
- Author's organization affiliation
- Date website or information was created

Websites that do not contain the author's name or title may have credibility issues, especially if the information contained therein cannot be corroborated with other websites. If the information is dated, it will obviously not contain the most up-to-date information. This could be a real issue. Again, if we use the example of pharmacist income used earlier, the $50,000 per year may have been accurate 15 years ago whereas the $100,000 per year income may be more reflective of what pharmacists currently make.

Using unreliable references will do at least two things, and neither of them will do you any favors. First and foremost you will express in writing invalid information. That leads to the second problem; at least while you are in school, and that is to guarantee that you will receive a low grade if in fact you are passing along bogus information. It is important to realize that your professors are experts in the field regarding what you are researching. They know what a good source is and in turn valid information when they see it! Therefore, it is important to always check at least two references when citing information.

Example of Choosing a Career Assignment

Career Path 1

Running Head: CAREER PATH

My Career Path to the World Bank

Joe Biology

Virginia Polytechnic Institute and State University

Assignment #4 for Biology Orientation Seminar (BIOL 1004)

Dr. Jack Evans, Instructor

10/13/10

Career Path 2

In today's society, global poverty is of huge concern, and many organizations are working to help developing countries and their people to alleviate that poverty. One of these organizations is the World Bank, which is located in Washington DC. The World Bank assembles and conducts many projects designed to improve living standards and reduce poverty. Last year, the World Bank provided $23.6 billion for 279 projects in developing countries worldwide. The projects are as diverse as providing microcredit in Bosnia and Herzegovina, raising AIDS-prevention awareness in Guinea, supporting educations of girls in Bangladesh, improving health care delivery in Mexico, and helping Timor to rebuild upon independence and India to rebuild Gujarat after a devastating earthquake (The World Bank Group, 2006).

After attending Virginia Tech and a chosen graduate School, I plan to work for the World Bank as a Project Coordinator/Director and be behind the scenes in many of the life-changing and heart-warming projects the bank conducts annually. From a day-to-day basis, I will design prospective projects and help direct the currently active ones. I will also be traveling abroad for extended periods, to oversee those projects. I will be responsible for making sure that the developing and poverty-stricken countries have plans by which to improve, and the means to do so.

Career Path 3

To achieve my goal of working for the World Bank, I must begin now by choosing the right courses and receiving above-average grades in those courses. It was recommended to me by Iaonnis Stivachtis, the Director of the International Studies Program here at Virginia Tech, to major in International Studies (concentrating on Global Development) while minoring in Spanish, Italian, and Arabic. To major in International Studies, it is required by Virginia Tech that you take two World Politic classes, Micro and Macroeconomics, International Relations Theory, International Law and Organization, and the Senior Seminar in International Studies. I must also take 12 credit hours of a foreign language, complete the VIEWS requirements, and take 9 credit hours of electives specific to the International Studies major (Saville, 2005).

It is recommended by the World Bank to have a Ph.D. in International Studies, and by my concentrating on Global Development, I will be preparing myself better for my prospective career. Wikipedia (2006) states that, "The World Bank's activities are focused on developing countries in fields such as human development, agriculture and rural development, infrastructure, and governance."

Career Path 4

Development concentration for the International Studies major will provide me all the necessary courses needed to prepare me for work in these areas.

The Graduate School that I plan to attend is Old Dominion University. My choice is based on their highly qualified and praised Graduate Program in International Studies. I will need to apply to Old Dominion University no later than mid-February to be considered for attending in the upcoming Fall semester. It is required to take the Graduate Record Exam and receive a minimum score of 1,200 on it and to have a 3.00 minimum cumulative GPA. Many other factors are involved in the competition for a seat in graduate school, but state residency is not one of them. The students admitted are chosen based on their academic success in their Undergraduate Programs and on the Examinations. After admittance, I will be able to obtain my PhD at Old Dominion University after 48 hours of course work, which will include at least 30 hours of dissertation. Also required for a PhD are the PhD Comprehensive Examination and the PhD Dissertations Guidelines Examination (Webmaster, 2006).

Career Path 5

Over the years, the workforce has become highly selective and competitive, and this applies to the World Bank as well. Given the highly selective process, a high GPA (3.7 to 4.0) is needed. Prior experience is also recommended, and many opportunities to gain that experience are provided by the World Bank through internships and programs such as Young Professionals, Junior Professional Associates, and Junior Officers. These programs help to give potential employees the background experience and knowledge needed to compete for a spot at the World Bank (The World Bank Group, 2006).

Despite all of the hard work required to achieve such a prestigious career, the time spent will be well worth it. With a starting salary of around $90,000 and many prospects for professional and salary advancement, I will barely think about the rough times I went through to make it that far (The World Bank Group, 2006).

In comparison to healthcare and education, International Studies is not in high demand. However, we must consider that the "Baby Boomers" are getting older and not enough young people of my generation are available to fill all of the gaps that the Boomers will leave behind. Based on that, just about every career will be in demand for new faces.

Career Path 6

International Studies was not always at the top of my list when it came to choosing a major and a career path. My father would hammer into my head ideas of becoming a lawyer or a doctor, and I actually listened to that advice until I came to Virginia Tech. I entered in August as a Biological Sciences major, with the goal of becoming an Obstetrician. My mind was quickly changed. I now know that it's not about what makes the most money, and it is not about an honorable title: It is all about loving what you do and doing what you love, and that is precisely what I will do by following my heart right to the World Bank. I want to make a difference in the world; I want to give children an education, clean water, care when they're sick, and the courage to make a difference in their own lives. I want to devote my life to making other lives better: This is my career path.

Career Path 7

References

Saville, R. (2006). Required Courses. *International Studies Major Requirements*. Retrieved October 10, 2010 from http://www.psci.vt.edu/internationalstudies/Major_Requirements.htm

The World Bank Group. (2006). Employment Opportunities. *The World Bank*. Retrieved October 7, 2010 from http://web.worldbank.org/WBSITE/EXTERNAL/

> EXTHRJOBS/0,,contentMDK:20522507~menuPK:64262363~pagePK:64262408~piPK:64262191~theSitePK:1058433,00.html
>
> Webmaster, A. (2005). Ph.D. in International Studies. *Old Dominion University: Graduate Program in International Studies.* Retrieved October 5, 2006 from http://al.odu.edu/gpis/phd/index.shtml
>
> Wikipedia. (2006). World Bank Group. *Wikipedia: The Free Encyclopedia.* Retrieved October 7, 2006 from http://en.wikipedia.org/wiki/World_Bank
>
> ***DO NOT USE WIKIPEDIA ! ! !***

APA Formatting

Reference List: Author/Authors

The following rules for handling works by a single author or multiple authors apply to all APA-style references in your reference list, regardless of the type of work (book, article, electronic resource, etc.)

Single Author

Last name first, followed by author initials.

EXAMPLE

Berndt, T. J. (2002). Friendship quality and social development. *Current Directions in Psychological Science, 11*, 7–10.

Two Authors

List by their last names and initials. Use the "&" instead of "and."

EXAMPLE

Wegener, D. T., & Petty, R. E. (1994). Mood management across affective states: The hedonic contingency hypothesis. *Journal of Personality & Social Psychology, 66,* 1034–1048.

Organization as Author

EXAMPLE

American Psychological Association. (2003).

Reference List: Electronic Sources

Article from an Online Periodical

Online articles follow the same guidelines for printed articles. Include all information the online host makes available, including an issue number in parentheses.

Author, A. A., & Author, B. B. (Date of publication). Title of article. *Title of online periodical, volume number* (issue number if available). Retrieved month day, year, from http://www.someaddress.com/full/url/

EXAMPLE:

Bernstein, M. (2002). 10 tips on writing the living Web. *A List Apart: For People Who Make Websites, 149*. Retrieved May 2, 2006 from http://www.alistapart.com/articles/writeliving

Nonperiodical Web Document, Web Page, or Report

List as much of the following information as possible; you sometimes have to hunt around to find the information; don't be lazy. If there is a page like http://www.somesite.com/somepage.htm, and somepage.htm doesn't have the information you're looking for, move up the URL to http://www.somesite.com/ If you cannot find an author, then write "Author unknown."

Author, A. A., & Author, B. B. (Date of publication). *Title of document*. Retrieved month date, year, from http://Web address.

APA Citation Basics

When using APA format, follow the author-date method of in-text citation. This means that the author's last name and the year of publication for the source should appear in the text, e.g., "(Jones, 1998)", and a complete reference should appear in the reference list at the end of the paper.

Summary or Paraphrase

When you are paraphrasing an idea or concept from another's work, you have to make reference only to the author and year of publication in your in-text reference, but APA guidelines encourage you to also provide the page number if you are providing information from a book source. It has been my experience over time that we have been trained in the Kindergarten through twelfth grade school system to provide quotes for the papers we have written. As a rule, we (scientists) ***do not quote*** from our sources or references, so please do not do this in your paper.

Potential Web Links
General Guides to Careers and Occupations

Virginia Tech Career Services

- www.career.vt.edu

America's Career Infonet:

- www.acinet.org/acinet/default.asp

Occupational Outlook Handbook:

- www.bls.gov/oco/

Employment Projections:

- http://stats.bls.gov

General Outlook on the US Job Market:

- www.acinet.org/acinet/oview.asp

Guide to Occupational Exploration (Berkeley):

- www.uhs.berkeley.edu/students/careerlibrary/links/career.cfm

Careers On-Line: Connect-Job Description Index:

- www.careersonline.com.au/show/jobs/index.html

Online Career Search:

- www.careerjournal.com

Job Factory:
- www.jobfactory.com

The Vault:
- www.vault.com/index.html

Human Resources & Employment:
- www.gov.ab.ca/hre

The American Institute of Biological Sciences:
- www.aibs.org

Specified Career Links

Aerospace Technician/Medicine
- www.nasa.gov
- www.utmb.edu/pmr/

Anesthesiologist
- www.lwwonline.com

Animal Caretaker
- www.wave.net/upg/immigration/dot_index.html
- www.oalj.dol.gov/libdot.htm
- www.nps.gov/training/npsonly/MNT/anmlcrtk.htm
- www.learnmoreindiana.org

Bioinformatics
- www.ebi.ac.uk

Biological Technician
- www.biosite.com
- www.bls.gov/ncs/ocs/ocsm/coma223.htm

Biology Teacher
- www.career.vt.edu

Biotechnologist
- www.umanitoba.ca/student/counselling/spotlights/biotechnology.html
- www.accessexcellence.org/AB/CC/bio_career_1.html
- www.genengnews.com
- www.ncbi.nlm.nih.gov/

Chiropractor
- www.chiropractor-finder.com

Clinical Data Specialist
- http://eahec.ecu.edu/telehealth/career10.html

Clinical Laboratory Scientist (Medical Technologist)
- www.uthscsa.edu/sah/cls/cls.html

Dentistry
- http://www.dentistry.vcu.edu/this_site/site_index.html

American Dental Association –
- http://stats.bls.gov/oco/ocos072.htm
- http://home.about.com/health/index.htm
- http://www.ada.org

Environment
- www.seedsguys.org
- http://www.cals.vt.edu

Forensic Science
- http://forensic.to/forensic.html
- www.fbi.gov/employment/employ.htm
- http://www.forensic-science-society.org.uk

Geneticist
- www.cc.umanitoba.ca/student/counselling/spotlights/genet.html

- http://biology.about.com/education/biology (Search for genetics)
- http://www.faseb.org/genetics/

Biological Law
- www.law.emory.edu
- www.environmental-law.net

Marine Biology/Ecology/Mammalogy
- http://life.bio.sunysb.edu/marinebio/mbweb.html
- http://www.seaworld.org/aquademics/tetra/bibliography.htm
- http://scilib.ucsd.edu/sio/guide/career.html
- http://www.ecology.com/
- www.marinecareers.net/index.php

Microbiologist
- www.asm.org

Optometry
- www.careeronline.com
- www.revoptom.com
- www.nei.nih.gov
- www.opted.org

Pathologist
- www.medsch.ucla.edu
- http://dir.yahoo.com/Health/Medicine/Pathology/

Pediatrician
- www.helpingyourchild.com
- www.aap.org

Pharmacy
- www.ashp.org
- http://www.aacp.org/
- http://www.pharmacytimes.com/

Physical Therapy
- www.apta.org (American Physical Therapist Homepage)
- http://pt.creighton.edu
- www.physicaltherapist.com

Physician

American Medical Association
- http://www.aamc.org
- http://www.acpe.org/

Physician's Assistant
- www.sempa.org
- www.aapa.org
- http://stats.bls.gov/oco/ocos081.htm

Employment Outlook for Veterinarians
- http://aavmc.org

Veterinary Medicine
- http://www.fda.gov/cvm/default.html

Virginia-Maryland Regional College of Veterinary Medicine
- www.vetmed.vt.edu

Virologist
- http://virology.wisc.edu/IMV/

Wildlife Biologist
- www.fw.vt.edu
- http://www.tpwd.state.tx.us/admin/

Zoologist
- http://www.princetonreview.com/Careers.aspx?page=1&cid=166&uidbadge=%07

Internships

Career Connect
- www.vipnet.org/collegejobs/index.html
- www.summerjobs.com

Aerospace
- www.nasajobs.nasa.gov

Animal Care Zoo
- www.santabarbarazoo.org/

Biomedical Research

World Health Laboratory
- www.training.nih.gov/student/sip/
- www.career.vt.edu/JOBSEARC/carsearch.htm

Botany
- www.dupont.com/careers/students/intern.html

Education
- www.dep.anl.gov

Environment
- www.ncseonline.org/
- http://www.ecojobs.com/environmental-internships.htm

Marine Biology/Ecology/Mammalogy
- www.aqua.org/internships/index.html
- www.odysseyexpeditions.org
- www.stanford.edu/dept/CDC/students/jobs/internships.html
- www.ocean.udel.edu/graduate/reu.html

Medical Internships
- http://summer.rpi.edu/update.do?artcenterkey=38

American Red Cross
- www.redcross.org/services/youth/0,1082,0_416_,00.html

Public Service
- www.rpi.edu/dept/sts/interns/
- www.twc.edu

Physical Therapy
- http://pt.creighton.edu/

Zoology
- www.getthatgig.com/cat_science.html

How to Achieve Your Goal
Your Academic Four-year Plan

The theme of this exercise is to weave together the requirements to graduate with a degree in Biological Sciences with the requirements for your career plan. The Academic Plan is not a plan that, once written, is cast in stone and cannot be modified. In actual practice, you will need to revisit and modify your plan, if necessary, each semester—asking the question, "Am I on track?" If your career plan changes, you will need to modify your four-year academic plan accordingly. If your GPA indicates that you are not going to be competitive in your career choice, then you need to modify both your career plan and your academic plan.

Issues to Consider

➤ What is the semester in which the course is taught (refer to catalog or departmental website)?

➤ What are the prerequisites for the courses planned for each semester?

➤ Do your biology electives reflect your career plan?

➤ What is the order in which courses should be taken from semester to semester?

While specific degree requirements will differ from institution to institution, the below information is relevant for students graduating with bachelor's degrees in science from the Department of Biological Sciences at Virginia Tech. As such, this is only an example, *as your degree requirements will surely differ at your chosen university.*

Grading Scheme for the Academic Plan Assignment

This is a very important tool that you will need to ensure that you will have completed all the requirements necessary for you to graduate from your chosen institution with a bachelor's degree in the Biological Sciences. If you, the student, properly plan the remaining time/coursework, two things are bound to happen. One, as already stated, you will have the roadmap necessary to complete your degree. Of equal importance, you will become, through proper planning of your courses, more attractive to those you are trying to impress! This includes, but is not limited to, potential graduate programs, professional schools (such as medical and dental schools), and of course, potential employers. Therefore, **your Academic Plan is of critical importance**.

You will be given the opportunity to complete your plan, and it will then be evaluated and returned with thoughtful suggestions that will strengthen it. You will then have the opportunity to revamp your four-year plan, as needed, and turn it in again. **Since it will be done, potentially, twice, I expect everyone to receive an A on this assignment**.

Grading Criteria for the Academic Plan

The grading scheme is fairly straightforward. Using your book and other available tools, you will create a plan in which you have all the necessary prerequisites to take a course in the semester that you plan to take it. For example, if you are planning to take a course entitled *Pathogenic Bacteriology*, you must have *already* taken the prerequisites for this course. If you have not taken these courses, then you will not be able to take *Pathogenic Bacteriology*.

Also, you must be aware of what semester each course is being offered. Semesters in which courses are offered are often times listed in the course catalogue of your institution and can also be found online. For example, if you choose to take an upper-division course, such as molecular biology, it is important that you are cognizant of which semester it is offered as well as what the prerequisites for the course are. Then, of course, you must plan accordingly.

Last, but not least, are typographical errors. As practicing scientists, you need to be highly critical, with painstaking attention to detail. Therefore, typographical errors are *unacceptable*; up to five points will be potentially taken off for each error!

Steps in Preparing an Academic Plan

1. List all required Biology, Chemistry, Physics, Math, and Statistics courses for the major, which can be found by referencing your check sheet.
2. List all courses you would like to take for University Curriculum for Liberal Education.

3. List all courses you would like to take for your biology electives.
4. Break down the list into semesters they are taught.
5. List prerequisites for courses and incorporate prerequisites into academic plan (e.g., you may want to take Mammalogy; if so, you need to make sure that you take Ecology prior to taking the course).
6. Begin to assemble your plan.

Examples of Required Biology Courses:

Course	Title	Prerequisites	Semester Taught
Biol 1105	Prin of Biology	N/A	Fall
Biol 1125	Biological Prin. Lab	N/A	Fall
Biol 1106	Prin of Biology II	N/A	Spring
Biol 1126	Biological Prin. Lab II	N/A	Spring
Biol 2004*	Genetics	Biol 1105, 1106	Fall & Spring
Biol 2104**	Cell & Molecular	Biol 1105, 1106	Fall & Spring
Biol 2704	Evolutionary	Biol 1105, 1106	Fall & Spring
Biol 2804	Ecology	Biol 1105, 1106	Fall & Spring
Biol 2604	Micro	Biol 1105, 1106 Chem 1035, 1036	Fall & Spring
Biol 2614	Micro Lab	Biol 1105, 1106, 1125, 1126, 2604	Fall & Spring

*BIOL 2004—Student should take BIOL 2104 and two semesters of General Chemistry before attempting this course.
**BIOL 2104 and 2004 should not be attempted during the same semester.

Example of Biology Electives that I Want to Take

Course	Title	Prerequisites	Semester Taught
Biol 3204	Plant Taxonomy & Lab	Biol 2304	Spring
Biol 3404	Intro Animal Physiology	Biol 2504, 2104	Spring
Biol 4434	Mammalogy & Lab	Either Biol 2504 or 2804	Fall
Biol 4534	Comparative Endocrinology	Biol 3404	Fall
Biol 4604	Food Micro & Lab	Biol 2604, 1614	Spring
Biol 4624	Microbial Genetics	Biol 2004, 2604	

Example of Core Courses I Want to Take for Core Requirements

Course	Title	Course	Title
Psyc 2004 Area 3	Intro Psychology	Psyc 2044 Area 3	Psychology of Learning
Hum 1704 Area 2	Intro Appalachian Studies	Phil 1204 Area 2	Knowledge and Reality
Hort 2164 Area 6	Floral Design	Ent 2004 Area 7	Insects and Human Society

Last Name _____   ID# _____

First Name _____

Fall Semester 2012				Spring Semester 2013			
Course	Number	Title	Hours	Course	Number	Title	Hours
		Total				Total	

Summer I 2013				Summer II 2013			
Course	Number	Title	Hours	Course	Number	Title	Hours
		Total				Total	

Fall Semester 2013				Spring Semester 2014			
Course	Number	Title	Hours	Course	Number	Title	Hours
		Total				Total	

Summer I 2014				Summer II 2014			
Course	Number	Title	Hours	Course	Number	Title	Hours
		Total				Total	

Fall Semester 2014					Spring Semester 2015			
Course	Number	Title	Hours		Course	Number	Title	Hours
		Total					Total	

Summer I 2015					Summer II 2015			
Course	Number	Title	Hours		Course	Number	Title	Hours
		Total					Total	

Fall Semester 2015					Spring Semester 2016			
Course	Number	Title	Hours		Course	Number	Title	Hours
		Total					Total	

Summer I 2016					Summer II 2016			
Course	Number	Title	Hours		Course	Number	Title	Hours
		Total					Total	

Academic Plan Example

Last Name _____Good_____   **ID#** _____000-00-0000_____

First Name _____I.B._____

Fall Semester 2009

Course	Number	Title	Hours
Biol	1004	Freshman Seminar	1.0
Biol	1105	Prin.Biol.Lect	3.0
Biol	1115	Prin.Biol.Lab	1.0
Chem	1035	Gen.Chem.Lect	3.0
Chem	1045	Gen.Chem.Lab	1.0
Engl	1105	Fresh. English	3.0
Math	1015	Elem.Calc.w/Trigl	3.0
		Total	**15**

Spring Semester 2010

Course	Number	Title	Hours
Biol	1106	Prin.Biol.Lect	3.0
Biol	1116	Prin.Biol.Lab	1.0
Chem	1036	Gen.Chem.Lect	3.0
Chem	1046	Gen.Chem.Lab	1.0
Engl	1106	Fresh English	3.0
Math	1016	Elem.Calcw/Trigl	3.0
Psych	2004	Intro.Psychology	3.0
		Total	**17**

Summer I 2010

Course	Number	Title	Hours
		Total	

Summer II 2010

Course	Number	Title	Hours
		Total	

Fall Semester 2010

Course	Number	Title	Hours
Chem	2535	Organic Chem.Lect	3.0
Chem	2545	Organic Chem.Lab	1.0
Biol	2604	Gen.Microbiol.Lect	3.0
Biol	2614	Gen.Microbio.Lab	1.0
Biol	2704	Evol. Biol	3.0
Math	2015	Elem.Calcw/TrigII	3.0
Psych	2054	Psych.of Personality	3.0
		Total	**17**

Spring Semester 2011

Course	Number	Title	Hours
Chem	2536	Organic Chem.Lect	3.0
Chem	2546	Organic Chem.Lab	1.0
Biol	2804	Ecology	3.0
Biol	2104	Cell and Molec.Biol	3.0
Lar	4034	Evol.Amer.Lands.	3.0
Stats	3615	Biol.Statistics	3.0
		Total	**16**

Fall Semester 2011				Spring Semester 2012			
Course	Number	Title	Hours	Course	Number	Title	Hours
Phys	2205	General Physics Lect	3.0	Phys	2206	General Physics Lect	3.0
Phys	2215	General Physics Lab	1.0	Phys	2216	General Physics Lab	1.0
Biol.	3014	Insect Biology Lect	3.0	Biol	2004	Genetics	3.0
Biol	3024	Insect Biology Lab	1.0	Engl.	2744	Intro.Creative Writ.	3.0
Engl.	3534	Literature and Ecol.	3.0	Biol.	3114	Field&Lab Ecol.	1.0
Geog	4074	Medical Geography	3.0	Biol	4354	Aquatic Entomol	3.0
xxx	xxxx	Vol. work in Field Lab		xxxx	xxxx	Vol.work Field Lab	
		Total	14			Total	14

Summer I 2012				Summer II 2012			
Course	Number	Title	Hours	Course	Number	Title	Hours
Biol	2504	General Zoology	3.0	Biol	2304	Plant Biology	3.0
		Total	3			Total	3

Fall Semester 2012				Spring Semester 2013			
Course	Number	Title	Hours	Course	Number	Title	Hours
Biol	4994	Undergrad.Res	3.0	Biol	4994	Undergrad.Res	3.0
Biol	4434	Mammalogy	4.0	Biol	4404	Ornithology	4.0
Biol	4004	Freshwater Ecol	4.0	Biol	3204	Plant Taxonomy	3.0
xxx	xxx	Free Elective	3.0	Geog	2314	Maps and Mapping	3.0
		Total	14			Total	13

Summer I 2013				Summer II 2013			
Course	Number	Title	Hours	Course	Number	Title	Hours
		Total				Total	

Who Am I—On Paper?
The Resume

At any given time, an opportunity may present itself, and you will be asked to supply information about yourself. This is the importance of the resume. As a freshman, you may think that developing a resume is not essential, but do not forget you should be thinking about summer internships, Co-op opportunities, undergraduate research opportunities, or summer jobs relevant to your career of interest. A resume is the professional way to leave something about you in the hands of a potential employer.

This exercise is intended to help you begin to develop a resume for professional opportunities. Two examples of resumes are included for your consideration. The first example is a resume of freshman biological sciences major. The second example is a resume of a graduating senior in the biological sciences major.

Pack Resume with Relevant Experience
Camille Wright Miller
Reprinted with permission of *The Roanoke Times*

In the course of my work, I see a lot of resumes. I talk with employers as they evaluate resumes. With recent college graduates or those about to graduate, employers don't expect to see a lengthy employment record.

Without a long employment record, though, employers must use other criteria to evaluate and sort resumes into the "yes," "maybe," and "no" piles. The selection criteria rarely are grade point average, major or the college attended.

For many employers, the most significant factor is the quality of the work experience the student or recent graduate has had. While a student may have to work to accumulate money for college, employers evaluate how that work experience relates to their business. Although a summer job may have provided the needed funds, if it isn't related to work the student wants to do upon graduation, there's less reason to move that resume to the "yes" pile.

For employers, the earlier a student demonstrates interest in a career field and provides evidence of the interest through jobs and internships, the stronger the student appears as a candidate for employment. A student completing his or her freshman year should look for internship opportunities in a field that interests the student.

If the internship is unpaid, the student may have to have a paying job to accumulate money for school. Dual employment–paid and unpaid–makes for a full summer but demonstrates to prospective employers that the student wanted hand-on experience in a chosen field.

The summers before the student's junior and senior years should demonstrate progressively stronger experience; projects, and exposure to the chosen field. By the summer before the senior year, the student generally should progress to the point where work in the chosen field is paid.

Beyond enhancing the resume, career-related experience can help students avoid costly and confidence-shattering experiences. I'm aware of more than on case where a student neared completion or completed a degree only to discover that what appealed on the academic side was unbearable when put into practice.

There was, for example, the student who was completing a degree in education. In the final semester of study, the student had to teach. In that situation, the student discovered that the student couldn't stand children.

To ensure high-quality internships and career-related experiences before graduation, college students should form strong partnerships with the college's career-development center. The career-development staff can point out existing opportunities, help create opportunities, and connect students to alumni in the desired field. They offer a student's first networking opportunity. They also have a number of assessment tools to help undecided students hone in on the right major for that student.

For those students who remain undecided about career choice, internships and career-related jobs offer opportunities to explore possibilities. While some of those experiences may not relate to the eventual career choice, they can be excellent points of discussion with an interviewer. One can say, "I thought I'd like a career in XYZ. My experience helped me understand that what I really want to do is ABC."

Experience is a strong selling point with many employers. The sooner one has the related experience, the stronger the resume, the more likely the "yes" pile.

Resume Example I

Sally R. Biology

Current Address:	**Permanent Address:**
2089 Derring Hall	222 Small Street
Virginia Tech	Blacksburg, VA 24134
Blacksburg, VA 24060	(540) 999-9999
(540) 231-9999	
biology@vt.edu	

OBJECTIVE	Lab assistant position related to zoology; interested in animal behavior
EDUCATION	**B.S., Biology, Expected May 2003** Virginia Tech, Blacksburg, VA

WORK EXPERIENCE	**Lead Supervisor, Retail Sales Hostess** • three gift shops at Busch Gardens • Williamsburg, VA • Summers 1998, 1999
	   Supervised and scheduled duties for cashiers
	   Handled cash transactions
	   Dealt with customers; handled complaints
	   Balanced tills; performed till runs
	   Organized, ordered, and restocked merchandise
	 Area Hostess • Busch Gardens • Williamsburg, VA • Summer 1997
	   Maintained park cleanliness
	   Interacted with guests
	   Operated children's rides

SKILLS	Teamwork and leadership Time management and organization Attention to detail and efficiency Punctuality
ACTIVITIES/HONORS	National Honor Society Mu Alpha Theta Girls' Tennis • Most Improved Player 1997 Multicultural Club • Treasurer SADD Spanish Club Debate Club

Resume Example II

Robert Biology
robert@vt.edu

Permanent Address: 2089 Derring Hall • Blacksburg, VA 24060 • (999) 999-9999

Objective

To pursue a position of SNP data analyst

Education

B.S. Biology with a concentration in Microbiology/Immunology; Minor in Chemistry: *May 2000*

VIRGINIA POLYTECHNIC INSTITUTE AND STATE UNIVERSITY, Blacksburg, VA

Study Abroad Exchange Program, Nice, France, *Fall 1999*

- Studied Management Principles, Microeconomics, Intermediate French, Music Appreciation
- Traveled to Italy, Switzerland, Germany, and France exploring a variety of cultures

Skills

- **Laboratory:** Aseptic Techniques, PCR, DNA purification, gel electrophoresis, centrifuge, thermocycler, DNA 3700 Sequencer, Tomtec, Titertek
- **Computer:** Windows 95, 98, NT, Microsoft Office 95, 97, 00, QuarkXPress, Adobe Products, Internet Applications, Q-Pulse, LDS 2.0, Exceed 7.1, Basic Unix commands, IBM, Macintosh
- **Certifications:** OSHA, Fire Extinguisher, CPR/AED, Document Control and SOP Retrieval, Black Belt in Tae Kwon Do
- **Language:** Proficiency in French

Work Experience

Celera Genomics, Rockville, Maryland:
Laboratory Technician I June 2000–current

- Worked on the Applera SNP Project, as a SNP scorer, by analyzing electrophoretic traces within a Unix-based environment
- Successfully completed and passed all examinations required for SNP scorers, and surpassed weekly quotas
- Provided laboratory support to R & D, QA/QC, and cDNA
- Maintained current production sequencing constantly striving to improve quality, success rate, and efficiency by following daily Standard Operating Procedures

- Helped reduce backlogs throughout the production pipeline in efforts to increase percentage of good data delivered to Celera's database
- Responsible for helping QC Validate a new version of Dye
- Trained several employees within Sequencing Chemistry, 3700 Sequencing, and SNP Scoring groups
- Recognized for my efforts in helping Celera meet deadlines for various genome projects
- Implemented 3700 troubleshooting techniques into the daily operations of the production lab

Auditing Assistant Trainer   **February 2001–September 2001**

- Assisted in auditing all labs for skill assessment, training needs, and equipment in the labs
- Worked as a team to develop training modules for various equipment uses in Production
- Developed training folders for employees to document required laboratory training
- Part of a team that organized a presentation on how to use various lab instruments

Microbiology Laboratory, Virginia Tech:
Laboratory Assistant/Undergraduate TA   **January 1999–May 2000**

- Prepared and organized lab chemicals and cultures, such as streak plates, gram stains, agar mediums
- Demonstrated knowledge and efficiency in using lab equipment, such as the autoclave, microscope, pipettes
- Assisted Graduate Teaching Assistant, during lab practical, by answering student questions

The Power of a Quality Resume

What is a Resume? Simply stated, this document briefly summarizes who you are and why you are the right person for the position in question. To do so, it will need to provide your contact information, as well as summarize your education, employment history, and your experiences. Generally speaking, your resume will contain the following: contact information, education, experience, honors, and activities. Your resume is a document designed specifically for you, by you. There are many styles of resumes, and you should choose one that you feel is a personal reflection of you. It is a marketing tool with the sole purpose of helping you get an interview. It will not get you the position you are applying for; rather, it will, if done well, allow you the opportunity for an interview.

What Resumes Should Include

- Your permanent address
- Your local or campus address
- Phone numbers for both local and permanent addresses
- Email addresses
- Your personal website, if you have one
- Education
- Experience
- Honors and activities

Resumes are designed to provide a snapshot of who you are and why you are the most qualified for the position at hand. Typically, resumes will only receive an initial look from your potential employer of approximately 45 seconds give or take.

There are some pitfalls that should be avoided at all costs.

1. Believe it or not, I see in resumes from time to time where students sometimes do not know the official name of their own university or college. I am a faculty member of Virginia Tech. The official name of Virginia Tech is Virginia Polytechnic Institute and State University. In reality, both of these two names are recognized and can be used interchangeably. I will see "The University of Virginia Tech," "Virginia Tech University," and the like on some of my students' resumes. Not knowing the name of the school that you have attended for four years is a sure-fire way to guarantee that you do not receive an interview!

2. People sometimes sell themselves short regarding their skills on the resume. For example, look at Robert Biology's resume experience relative to his **Laboratory Technician I**. It is well done and gives the reader great insight into his abilities and experiences in the lab. If, on the other hand, he had written only that he had worked with DNA procedures, the reader would have a very incomplete view of his capabilities. This, in turn, would translate into him not getting an interview for the position of SNP data analyst!

3. People submit a resume with typographical errors, and trust me, it only takes one to get your resume thrown right in the trash! This, my friends, will not do you any favors. Prior to my current position as a professor, I was an Environmental Consultant. One of my many job duties was to manage our laboratory. As such I was charged with hiring new staff members in my laboratory. With that said, I saw literally hundreds of resumes for each new position. The very first thing I would do is read each resume looking for typographical errors.

You guessed it—every resume with a typo went straight into my trash can, and of course, whoever wrote it was not asked for an interview. My reasoning was quite simple. If the applicant could not even present me with a resume devoid of typos, that person was not capable of working in my laboratory, which had scientific machinery that literally cost hundreds of thousands of dollars. So, providing a potential employer of graduate school with a resume that is not accurate and precise sheds some light on how a person might function in my lab or in graduate school. When you create a resume, it is imperative to make sure that everything is accurate and precise. That is what scientists do.

In order to make sure that your resume says everything you want it to say, you should take advantage of all the resources at your disposal. Have several of your colleagues read over it, take it to the writing center, and go to your career Services on campus; they will have experts whose job is to help you create a personal resume that will help you get the interview for a job or graduate or professional school.

I am often asked by my students whether their resumes should be confined to one or two pages. The answer is that it all depends. I have colleagues who have resumes (Curriculum Vitae, also known as a CV) as long as 45 pages! So, the length of your resume or CV all depends on your experiences to date. Typically, young people in college or newly graduated have resumes that are one or two pages in length based on their experiences to date.

FREQUENTLY ASKED QUESTIONS

- **How can I find out who my adviser is?**

   If you forget who your advisor is, check your account at your institution or contact the advising office at your institution.

- **How do I switch advisors?**

   If, for any reason, you decide you would like to switch your advisor, contact the advising office within your department.

- **What if I want to take a class, but the class is full? Can I force-add the class?**

   Often, your institution will have a method for adding students to courses that appear full. Again, contact your advising department or the professor teaching the course to see what the possibilities are of being added to the course you would like to take in a given semester.

- **What do I need to do if I want to take classes elsewhere?**

   Your institution will have a policy in place regarding this issue. Often, you will need to fill out an "Authorization to Take Courses Elsewhere" form. A copy of this form typically can be found on the university website. If not, you should contact your advisor.

- **I would like to change my major what do I do?**

   A student in the College of Science typically can freely change into another major. With that said, there are times that certain majors have restricted access. Again, this information can readily be found on the university website. For information on transferring into a restricted major, contact the department in question.

   Students wishing to change into a major in another College must meet any prerequisites that the College and Departments have. Students should obtain the "Change of Major/Minor Form" from the new Dean's Office. The new Dean, the former Dean, the former advisor, and the new advisor must sign this form. It is turned in to the new Dean's Office.

- **When do I have to declare a major and or minor?**

   Each institution potentially is different regarding the timeframe in which students must declare a major. Typically, students must be enrolled in a major by the start of their junior year (before they reach 90 hours) to graduate in that major. Again, this information should be readily available on the university website. If not, certainly your advisor will have the answer to this question.

➤ **How many hours do I need to graduate?**

Again, this information will be specific to your university and, potentially, your chosen major. This information should be available on the university website, or it can be obtained from your advisor.

➤ **How do I calculate my GPA?**

Calculating Your GPA

Here are some brief answers to the "how to" questions students most often ask their advisors. They are included here so that you can have the "nuts and bolts" information for easy reference. It is still a good idea to consult your academic advisor if you have questions about your GPA. HokieSpa provides an electronic version of this calculator.

Step 1

Multiply the number of credit hours for each class by the number of "quality credit (QC) points" earned for the grade you receive: A=4, A−=3.7; B+=3.3, B=3.0, etc. (A "plus" or "minus" is .3 more or less than its letter grade.) For a three-credit class in which you earn an A, for example, give yourself 12 points.

Step 2

Once you have arrived at the total quality credit points for each class, add them all together.

Step 3

Divide the total quality credit points by the number of credit hours you passed that were graded A to F, plus the number of credit hours you failed, whether graded A to F or P/F. **(Pass-fail classes that you fail count in your GPA, but pass-fail hours that you pass do not.)**

This would be your GPA if these were the grades you earned in these six courses:

	Grade	=	QC points	×	Credit hours	=	Total QC points
Step 1	A	=	4.0	×	3	=	12.0
	C	=	2.0	×	3	=	6.0
	C+	=	2.3	×	3	=	6.9
	B+	=	3.3	×	1	=	3.3
	D−	=	0.7	×	3	=	2.1
	F	=	0.0	×	3	=	0.0
Step 2					16		30.3
Step 3			Total QC	÷	Total Credit Hours	=	GPA
			30.3	÷	16		1.893

How would a grade of F affect my grade in a course taken P/F?

Step 1

Total all hours attempted A/F **plus** P/F hours **failed**

Step 2

Quality Credits earned/letter grade

Step 3

Divide Total Quality Credits earned by Total Hours Attempted from step 1 = GPA

Grades with a P/F course Failed

	Grade	=	QC points	×	Credit hours	=	Total QC points
	A	=	4.0	×	3	=	12.0
	C	=	2.0	×	3	=	6.0
	C+	=	2.3	×	3	=	6.9
	B+	=	3.3	×	1	=	3.3
	D–	=	0.7	×	3	=	2.1
P/F	F	=	0.0	×	3	=	0.0
					16		30.3
			Total QC	÷	Total Credit Hours	=	GPA
			30.3	÷	16		1.893 **You are on probation**

Grades with a P/F course passed

	Grade	=	QC points	×	Credit hours	=	Total QC points
	A	=	4.0	×	3	=	12.0
	C	=	2.0	×	3	=	6.0
	C+	=	2.3	×	3	=	6.9
	B+	=	3.3	×	1	=	3.3
	D–	=	0.7	×	3	=	2.1
	P	=		×	3	=	0.0
					16		30.3
			Total QC	÷	Total Credit Hours	=	GPA
			30.3	÷	13		2.3308

What GPA do I need to earn this term to have the overall GPA I want at the end of the term?

+   Hours that count in your GPA as of the end of last semester (all courses taken A/F plus any P/F courses that you failed)

    Hours you are taking this semester that you will count in your GPA

=   Total hours (that will count in your GPA at the end of this semester to have that overall GPA)

×   GPA that you want at the end of this semester

=   Number of Quality Credits you will need at the end of this semester to have that overall GPA

−   Number of Quality Credits you have already earned (see grade report or course history summary)

=   Number of Quality Credits you will need to earn this semester to reach the GPA you want.

÷   Hours you are taking this semester

=   GPA you need to earn this semester to reach the overall GPA you want

CPSIA information can be obtained at www.ICGtesting.com
Printed in the USA
LVOW01s1033150715

445481LV00005B/13/P